"*Loyalty Marketing: The Second Act* is the new bible for customer-focused retailers worldwide."
— **Frank Murphy,** Director, Superquinn

"Brian Woolf, whose first book, *Customer Specific Marketing* lifted the veil on the secrets of successful loyalty marketing and changed the industry, has done it again! His thoughts on *threshold measurements* alone are worth more than even his always-valuable seminars. Read this book before your competitors do."
— **Fred Newell,** Author of *loyalty.com* and *Wireless Rules*

"Brian's Woolf's new book is certainly the most fascinating, comprehensive, and readable coverage of retail loyalty programs in the world today. It is filled with specific examples taken from a variety of companies in many countries. It explains clearly the advantages of discounts vs points, plus what use can be made of the valuable data gained from a loyalty program. No one in retailing should try to run his business without reading this book."
— **Arthur Middleton Hughes,** Vice President for Strategic Planning, msdbm, Los Angeles and author of *The Complete Database Marketer* and *Strategic Database Marketing*

"What is so valuable about Brian Woolf's new book is that it shows us how to measure and manage customers' behavior— something missing in other marketing books which typically talk more about general concepts."
— **Luis Martinez,** Director of Marketing, Dia, Madrid, Spain

"Inspiring case studies. Actionable ideas. Fundamental rules. Measurable reports. Whether you are just getting started or are well down the path of loyalty marketing, you will find *The Second Act* indispensable."
— **Scott Ukrop,** Vice President of Marketing, Ukrop's Super Markets, Richmond, Virginia

"In this book Brian Woolf has given even advanced practitioners of loyalty marketing a set of global best practices against which they can judge and then improve their own performance."
— **Kevin Doris,** CEO, Gerland's, Houston, Texas

"Brian Woolf's new book is wonderful! It offers insight into the minds of some of CRM's best retailers, and how their attitudes toward customers changed as they learned to use data. As an added bonus, these leaders share some of their most creative and effective ideas. The book is filled with rules of thumb, easy-to-follow models, and real-life bottom line results. If everyone followed this advice, we would see no more failed loyalty marketing programs. Anyone who wants to learn about the current CRM masters, or hopes to become one, needs to read this book."
— **Carlene Thissen,** President, Retail Systems Consulting, Naples, Florida

"It's all about the data – and what you do with it. *Loyalty Marketing: The Second Act* lays it all on the table. Replete with demonstrable stories of the world's best practices in loyalty card marketing, Brian Woolf leads you down a path towards the mastery of your own program. You'll enjoy his conversational style of writing and come away with a new vision. Read it with a highlighter, change colors, and then read it again."
— **Bill Roth,** CEO, Pervasive Marketing Group, Denver

"A major strength of the book is its use of example after example of strategies used by successful retailers in ways that let everyone know not only 'what can be done', but that 'it can be done' successfully."
— **Earl Johnson,** Director of Marketing, Hardin Piggly Wiggly, Gadsden, Alabama

"This is an excellent read. While there are some more technical chapters, Brian's manner of writing makes it interesting and entertaining instead of scholarly and dry."
— **Cathleen Jacobson,** Director, Marketing & Print Media, Carson Pirie Scott & Co., Milwaukee, Wisconsin

"The problem with most loyalty programs is not the plastic cards but the 'plastic' programs! Here's an authoritative book about the numbers and key factors that add up to make an exciting and profitable program for customers, retailers and suppliers."
— **Gordon Cooper,** Director, The Continuity Company, Italy

———

SOME USES OF CUSTOMER INFORMATION

LOYALTY MARKETING

~ *The Second Act* ~

BRIAN WOOLF

Library of Congress Cataloging-in-Publication Data
2001 135329

ISBN: 0-9632025-4-5
1. Marketing. 2. Management

WOOLF, BRIAN P.
Loyalty Marketing: The Second Act

ALSO BY BRIAN WOOLF
Customer Specific Marketing © 1996
Shrinking the Corporate Waistline © 1992

Printed in the United States of America

Published by Teal Books, 6 Parkins Lake Court, Greenville, SC 29607-3628
Tel: (864) 458-8277   Fax: (864) 458-8144   Eml: books@brianwoolf.com

Distributed by Raphel Marketing, 118 S. Newton Place, Atlantic City, NJ 08401
Tel: (609) 348-6646   Fax: (609) 347-2455   Eml: info@raphel.com

Managing Editor: Don J. Beville

Book Jacket & Text Design: Dennis Michael Stredney
                           Stredney Design Graphic Solutions
                           Richmond, Virginia

~ To order additional copies, please turn to back of book ~

Second Printing 2006

To my wife, Marie,
&
my daughter, Fiona

APPRECIATION

My warmest thanks to two very special people who were of significant help in the development of this book:

Wanda Shive, a business colleague who makes database numbers coherent and transforms them into meaningful reports

Robin Clark, a wise and friendly critic who made my tortured syntax and grammar relax and fall quietly into place

The purpose of this book is to help those with a loyalty program build upon the foundation that has already been laid. Three themes, interwoven throughout the book, are used to accomplish this. They are set out below.

The book may be read in one of two ways. Either the traditional way, from cover to cover, or by moving through it theme by theme. To follow the second path, turn to the Introduction after reading this section. There you will learn the book's background and goals. Next, scan the Contents to see what the book covers and how it's laid out. Then delve into whichever theme piques your curiosity the most. This can readily be done as the chapters are largely self-contained and ideas relating to earlier chapters are clearly referenced. Whichever route you choose, I hope you enjoy the journey.

THREE MAIN THEMES

1. Information and measurement is essential for success

The great value of a loyalty card program lies in its information. How to use this information is all-important, so practical examples are included. This theme is covered in the following chapters:

2. Role models for success

We gain confidence in a new course of action when we see it successfully practiced elsewhere. What are the best retailers doing with their loyalty programs? How are they doing it? Why are their leaders so committed to their programs? This theme is covered in the following chapters:

3. Key ideas underpinning loyalty marketing

As with most things in life, there are certain rules for achieving success. Understanding and practicing them helps make success more likely. What are some of these rules and essential elements that we need to know in this arena? You will find the key ideas underpinning loyalty marketing covered in the following chapters:

CONTENTS

CONTENTS *(continued)*

INTRODUCTION

THE SECOND ACT

Most *Failures Come in the Second Act.* In this thoughtful article in *International Trends in Retailing* (Fall, 1989), Michael J. O'Connor, one of retailing's foremost observers over the past forty years, reminds us that simply attracting new customers to our "show" is not enough. We need to have a great Second Act to keep them in their seats.

Loyalty marketing is no different. Sales and profit gains are almost always assured in the First Act, when stale and inefficient promotional practices are replaced with freshly packaged offerings. Impressive gains have been made. From diverse parts of the world, retailers have proudly shared with me their First Act successes:

❖ *Since the birth of our card program, we have seen a significant jump in our gross profit percentage.*

❖ *Our gross profit percentage is now 2% higher than it was last year.*

❖ *In the 10-12 weeks since launching our card, same-store sales are up 9% over trend.*

❖ *We increased our sales 12% and our operating profit by 100% in the first full year of our program.*

❖ *We had a great first year. For a billion dollar retailer, to increase same-store sales by 5% and profits by more than 30% in our launch year is very exciting.*

❖ *Not only are sales at a record level after four quarters, but our gross profit percentage is at a record level too.*

However, results of loyalty card programs in the years immediately following the launch year—the Second Act— vary greatly. Those with a great Second Act have told me:

❖ *We are in the second year of our program. Our bottom line profit in the latest quarter is up 74% over last year. This surge of profitability is allowing us to increase our store count 10 to 20% this year.*

❖ *This is the fourth year of our program. Sales in the last nine months are up 14% and profits are up 25%.*

❖ *Our gross profit percentage is up 1.5% over last year and we expect it to increase another 0.5% by year-end.*

❖ *We are expecting a profit increase of well over 50% this year—on top of last year's jump.*

❖ *We have increased the number of our $100+ per week customers over the past two years by 87%.*

❖ *In three of the last four years, we have had double-digit, same-store sales growth. The last two years, in particular, have been extraordinary and fantastic for us. As a result we are on a roll and plan to open a lot more stores over the next couple of years while we have such great momentum.*

Others who launched a loyalty card program but didn't write a great script for their Second Act—or who performed their script poorly—have been disappointed. Some have even abandoned their programs. Alas, both Broadway and Main Street have their share of failures!

THE GOALS OF THIS BOOK

One key goal of this book is to describe the requirements for success in the Second Act. In addition to showing why certain companies are enjoying a great Second Act, a review of their First Acts will be covered. We will even peek behind the curtain to discover what some loyalty leaders think about their programs and of companies without one.

Another goal of the book is to answer some of the more pithy questions asked of me in recent years:

1. What are global best practices?
2. Why have some programs failed?
3. How should we measure success?
4. What are the common denominators of success?
5. Are some programs inherently better than others?
6. What keeps customers interested in the program?
7. Why don't all retailers embrace loyalty marketing?
8. How deeply should a loyalty program permeate a company?

The responses are drawn from my experiences around the world helping retailers with the planning, launching, operating, critiquing, refining, and/or restructuring of their loyalty card programs. Companies with whom I have had the privilege of working cover the gamut of retailing: from hard discounters to hypermarkets; from self-service to high service; from independent retailers to global chains. The lessons learned are relevant not just to retailers, both off-line and on-line, but also to practitioners of loyalty marketing in all sectors.

This book follows two earlier works relating to loyalty marketing: *Measured Marketing: A Tool to Shape Food Store Strategy,* and *Customer Specific Marketing.*

The former was a major 6-month research report I was invited to undertake in 1993 for the Coca-Cola Retailing Research Council. Its purpose was to explain the successes, failures, and lessons of supermarket loyalty card programs in the preceding five years.

The latter, a book published in 1996, built upon the foundations laid in the previous study and shows readers how to successfully introduce and run a loyalty program.

Since *Customer Specific Marketing* was published there have been numerous new insights in the loyalty arena. Five major ones, which you will read about in this book, are:

1. A loyalty program's greatest benefit is the information

2. Points programs costing 1% of sales are questionable

3. Best Customers are the critical success indicator

4. Charging a membership fee makes great sense

5. There's no single best strategy

WHAT IS LOYALTY MARKETING?

Loyalty is a positive attitude built up over a series of favorable interactions and is expressed in a customer's behavior. Therefore, loyalty marketing is doing well *all* of those things that influence the perception of our customers, resulting in them shopping more regularly with us.

Loyalty marketing is not new. It has been practiced since the birth of retailing. Friendly service and clean stores, along with an enticing assortment of quality products at fair prices, have always been key business differentiators. Those retailers who best executed this combination of service-cleanliness-assortment-quality-price generated more repeat business (ie, more loyalty) than their competitors.

It's important to understand that *loyalty card marketing* is just one element of loyalty marketing, even though the two are often confused. Loyalty marketing involves much more than just a card.

The primary purpose of a loyalty card is to capture customer data to help us better understand our customers' behavior. The card also has two important secondary roles: it acts both as an identification vehicle and a triggering device for unique customer offers and rewards.

A loyalty card is not something that, once introduced, automatically increases customer loyalty. The information it generates increases our customer knowledge, allowing us to make better decisions across many areas of the company— not just marketing—resulting in improved sales and profits.

Therefore, a loyalty card is not a replacement for any of the basic loyalty drivers but is a supplement to them. Just as a hammer doesn't build a house, a loyalty card doesn't build customer loyalty. Both the hammer and the card are tools that, when properly and appropriately used, help bring the architect's blueprint to life.

A PRAGMATIC BUSINESS-BUILDING TOOL

A loyalty card program, as it moves through its Second Act, proves to be a pragmatic, business-building tool. It measures customer behavior and relates it directly to bottom-line results.

Paradoxically, loyalty marketing has a bias towards customers who, say, spend $50 per week but who are only 50% loyal, rather than towards those who spend $10 per week and claim to be 100% loyal. This is because the higher spender yields greater returns.

The information from loyalty cards is powerful—that's why today's leaders are collecting over 80% of their sales from their card members.

FUZZY LOYALTY

If you ask the CEOs of companies in any industry about the role of customers in their business, almost all will tell you that customers are at their core. Some will quote Drucker or Levitt, explaining that the purpose of their business is to retain and add customers. Others will quote their mission statement, explaining that customers are the sun around which their business world revolves.

Then follow up with clarification questions, such as:

- Given that customers are at the heart of your business, how do you define and measure customer success?
- How do you measure customer activity? Customer profitability?

❖ Do you differentiate between customers and shoppers or between best and potential best customers?

❖ How do you communicate your customer performance throughout the whole company?

❖ How do you reward your employees for improvements in performance of this central focus of your business?

With a loyalty card program, a retailer can now answer these questions. Without one, the answers are merely guesswork.

THE INTERNET

The Internet is one of many important tools to help retailers achieve their corporate strategy. However, just as there was no need in the past for businesses to have a telephone, radio, television, or fax strategy, there is no need today for an "Internet strategy". All are simply devices to help us communicate more effectively with customers. As with the earlier inventions, this new technology should be a seamless part of the business. Internally, Internet transactions should be part of the same financial records and corporate customer database as the rest of the company. We must always keep in mind that the Internet is but another customer touchpoint and should be treated accordingly.

A retailer's Internet site has the same characteristics as a store. It should be easy to enter, move around in, and exit; "signage" should be clear and attractive; and "someone" should always be available to answer customers' questions. Addressing these fundamentals will go a long way to meet customers' primary needs.

Having said that, on-line retailers with loyalty programs will find this book very instructive as loyalty principles apply equally to on-line and off-line businesses. The reports showing how to measure success can be used by any business with customers and the discussion on points and their economics will be of particular value.

A NOTE ON STYLE

One stylistic comment is necessary. In a book of this nature there will be a constant reference to customers and retailers who, obviously, are both male and female. How should they be described? Should the term "he", "she", or "he (she)" be used to describe either? The usually versatile English language fails us in this regard. For reading ease, where I have not been able to devise a suitable neutral phrasing, I have elected to use feminine descriptors for customers, as the majority of retail customers are women, and male descriptors for retailers, using similar reasoning.

In addition, throughout the book are a number of explanatory tables. To make it easier for you to compare your performance with the company being described, as well as to protect its identity, most tables are expressed in terms of 10,000 households. You can benchmark your results with those in the example by simply converting your data to the same base.

THE LOYALTY JOURNEY

The myriad ways available to make different offers to our diverse customers provide great opportunities for retailers to become even more customer-centric. There are so many paths to choose. We are on an exciting journey. Every day our experiences and observations generate fresh ideas and new insights—yet we all still have so much learning ahead.

As you move down your unique loyalty path, you will discover new approaches and may have different results to those described in this book. If you would care to share them, please e-mail me at bpw@brianwoolf.com

It would be a pleasure to hear from you.

REQUENTLY USED TERMS IN THIS BOOK

DROP'N: Diamonds, Rubies, Opals, Pearls and New customers. A customer hierarchy. In this book, Diamonds typically spend >$100 per week, Rubies $50-100, Opals $25-50, Pearls <$25.

BEST CUSTOMERS (BCs): The highest spending customer group; eg, Best Customers among US food retailers spend over $50 per week, on average, in a quarter (ie, they are the Diamonds and Rubies).

POTENTIAL BEST CUSTOMERS (PBCs): Customers who are neither Best nor New Customers (ie, they are the Opals and Pearls).

KEY CUSTOMERS (KCs): Diamond, Ruby, and Opal customers (ie, those spending over $25 week).

ACTIVE CUSTOMER: A customer who shops at least once in the period under review.

INACTIVE CUSTOMER: A customer who has shopped in a prior quarter, but not in the current quarter.

REACTIVATED CUSTOMER: A customer who did not shop in the previous quarter, but returns to shop in the current quarter.

NEW CUSTOMER: A customer who shops for the first time in the quarter. (She is identified by the first use of her loyalty card.)

PRE-EXISTING ACTIVE CUSTOMERS (PEAs): Those who shopped (ie, were active) last quarter and shopped again this quarter.

SIGNATURE ITEM: An item of distinctive taste or quality that a retailer offers; the identical item is not sold by competitors.

BOY, EOY: Beginning of year, End of year.

HHPR: Household Penetration Rate

P.W.: Per week.

PTW: Per Trading Week. Example: a 10-store chain in a 4-week period has 40 trading weeks in that period.

Q OR QTR: Quarter.

SPV: Spend Per Visit (ie, average transaction size).

SPW: Spending Per Week (ie, average spending per week).

VPW: Visits Per Week (ie, avg. number shopping visits in week).

FIGURE 1: FREQUENTLY USED TERMS

PART I

AN INTRODUCTION TO EXCELLENCE

Chapter 1: A Tale of Two Cities

Excellence in action

Two retailers demonstrate that customer loyalty comes from a great loyalty card program, and a whole lot more.

Chapter 2: Customer Churn and Burn

Why excellence is needed

A case study that shows us how much customer churn and burn one leading retailer experienced. We see how much the often undetected ebb and flow of customers affects results and what measurements we can use to begin reducing our own customer outflow.

Chapter 3: From Deciles to Thresholds

How excellence is measured

This chapter provides an introduction to effective customer measurement. Also presented is a practical alternative to the decile segmentation of customers used by direct marketers, in the form of threshold reports.

A TALE OF TWO CITIES

Chapter 1

It has been my experience that the CEOs whose first priorties are customers and employees tend to run more stable and more profitable companies in the long run.

... Michael J. O'Connor

In the best of times, in the worst of times, they believed in loyalty marketing. Business fads came, business fads went, but their customers were first, last, and always. Both before and after they introduced their loyalty card programs, their goal was the same: to understand their customers, to please them, and to encourage them to return.

Dayton and Dublin. Two distinctly different cities, each with a unique customer-centric retailer: Dorothy Lane Market in Dayton and Superquinn in Dublin; each company with a world-class loyalty program.

Before the introduction of their loyalty card programs, their customer-building decisions were decided in that gray haze of intuition aided by anonymous transaction data. With the launch of their loyalty card programs, their decision-making was radically enriched by customer-specific data. A new epoch in retailing had dawned for them both.

Their early steps towards a loyalty card program were cautious—neither wanted to offend any customer. Norman Mayne, the CEO of Dorothy Lane, was so anxious that the night before the program's launch, he called his director of loyalty marketing to see if its introductory newspaper advertisement could be pulled. "Don't worry," he was assured, "if it doesn't work, we can go back to our old ways in 4-6 weeks." Two years earlier, Superquinn had quietly offered its program to its existing customers for five months before its public launch.

In the first year of each program, both companies modestly increased their same-store sales—and materially increased their same-store profits—over prior trends. *Customer knowledge had quickly yielded better returns than intuition and guesswork.*

What do these two companies have in common? They've always been customer focused and both are led by passionate, visionary merchants seeking to provide a superior shopping experience. Rather than become "general stores", as have many supermarkets, they concentrate on food. Their point of differentiation in their respective marketplaces is that they are the "food specialists".

With the assurance that comes with greater customer knowledge, both have distanced themselves further from competitors and have enjoyed even greater prosperity since their loyalty card programs began. Not entirely because of their loyalty cards, but partly so—the card has simply helped them do what they were doing before, but now even better. Better information has led to better decision-making across the whole business.

The customer-focused goals of these two companies are similar, yet they have taken different paths to success. Let's discover what makes their "shows" special.

DOROTHY LANE MARKET AND CLUB DLM

Surrounded in Dayton, Ohio, by three of the best retail giants in the US—Kroger, Cub Foods, and Meijer—Dorothy Lane Market exemplifies how an independent operator can thrive. Over fifty years old, with just two stores, it has built a reputation far beyond its size. Customers from all over North America are drawn to its website, dorothylane.com, to order two of its more famous store-differentiating *signature items,* Heavenly Ham® and its delightfully decadent Killer Brownies. Locals log on to order deliveries of its avant-garde (taste-wise) box lunches. *Club DLM* members access the site for special weekly deals, upcoming events (eg, a Sausage Cookout or the annual Diaper Derby), to search its well-organized Recipe Archives for ideas, or to enroll for Dorothy Lane's next School of Cooking.

Dorothy Lane is a Mecca for food aficionados or "foodies". In addition to their regular weekly groceries, foodies also accomplish their goal of locating the widest selection of olive oils, fine wines, tasty breads, bakery items, gourmet cheeses, fresh produce, and premium quality meats. Foodies are also tempted by unique offerings such as Artisan hearth-baked baguettes, shiny Alaskan salmon, and comforting lattes.

This unique company is also renowned for its friendly, helpful service in every department, where every customer is greeted with a warm smile. To me, Dorothy Lane Market is the "Harrods of the MidWest" in food retailing.

So how then does a loyalty card fit into such a distinctive operation? Indeed, why even consider the idea? We will now find out.

THE FIRST ACT

After *Club DLM's* apprehensive launch in May 1995, the lessons—and changes—came quickly. By making all promotionally priced items available only when a *Club DLM* card was presented, regular customers readily enrolled giving the company its first concrete insights into their behavior.

The first two months of data convinced Norman Mayne and his team that Dorothy Lane Market served a wide variety of customers. They ranged from those who were attracted primarily by the company's advertised weekly specials—the "cherry pickers"—to its fabulous foodies.

Believing that the future lay more with the latter than the former, the company set off down an unknown and—for retailers—fearful path. Just three months after the card's debut, Dorothy Lane eliminated its weekly newspaper advertisement. It was replaced—with appropriate customer notice—with an in-store "hot sheet" featuring similar items, but at even lower prices. This 180-degree change in its promotional strategy worked! Sales held. Profits rose.

Its radical decision vindicated, the company refined its communication program one step further by launching a monthly *Market Report*. This eight-page newsletter with food news, recipes, and activities at Dorothy Lane also included a page featuring either six or eight coupons, valid throughout the coming month. The *Market Report* (which continues today as a key element of the company's marketing strategy) was mailed to approximately the top thirty percent of its *Club DLM* members (who provide 75% of its sales). But with one twist: recipients were divided into three groups, each group being offered a different price for the same item, with the lowest priced coupons being offered to the highest spending group. A customer-sensitive retailer, who previously had believed in treating every customer equally, had now fully embraced differentiated marketing.

Over time, as the *Market Report* coupon specials were priced even more aggressively for these better customers, the company financed these deeper markdowns by slowly trans-forming its generally available in-store hot sheet into a less aggressively priced "lukewarm" sheet. Dorothy Lane had evolved from an "all customers are equal" marketing strategy into a Best Customer strategy where the focus was on rewarding, retaining and building the number of its higher spending customers.

Did Dorothy Lane lose customers in this first year? Yes. Transactions declined as the price-oriented shoppers—the cherry pickers—could no longer compare its prices with competitors' ads while sitting at their kitchen tables. Yet sales and profits increased as Dorothy Lane devoted more of its efforts and rewards towards its regular, better customers. Norman Mayne recently stated that within 18 months of its card launch, Dorothy Lane's annual profits had doubled compared to those in the twelve months prior to launch!

"It was like a blinding flash of the obvious," he explained. For years he had tried to look after every customer fairly— yet not all customers treated his company fairly in return. He now sought a more balanced relationship. Some customers, he discovered, made so much noise yet contributed so little to the business. From the reassurance he gained from the data, he realized that he no longer had to "do gymnastics to keep some of them." The information his loyalty card generated had moved him from theory and uncertainty to reality and confidence.

REWARDING CUSTOMER BEHAVIOR

What is unique about Dorothy Lane's approach to loyalty marketing is its emphasis on rewarding customers for past behavior. "It's all about integrity and trust," Mayne told me. "It's an insult to a good customer to say to her, 'Spend $x in the next 10 weeks and you'll receive a reward,' when she has already shown how valuable she is during the past quarter or past year. When we ask good customers to jump through future hoops, we are telling them that what they have spent in the past doesn't count. But I know my good customers from my database. I'm just going to look after them."

An excellent illustration of this principle in action is seen each year at Thanksgiving. US supermarkets that don't have loyalty cards indulge in kamikaze pricing of turkeys, often promoting them at $0.39 per pound, although it costs them almost twice that. In contrast, many supermarkets with loyalty cards skew the offer in favor of their regular, more profitable customers with an offer along these lines: "Spend $500 in the 10 weeks before Thanksgiving and we'll give you a free turkey; or spend $250 and we'll give you a certificate for $5 off your turkey. Otherwise, it's available at the regular price."

Dorothy Lane's approach is different, even from that of the typical loyalty card operator. All turkeys are offered at full price in its stores. However, a few weeks prior to Thanksgiving, three versions of a surprise "thank-you" letter are mailed to its better customers. The letter thanks them for being loyal customers and invites them to accept an enclosed gift certificate. Depending on the customer's spending history, the certificate is for a free turkey or for $10 or $5 off a turkey of their choice. To Dorothy Lane, these are rewards to customers who have already shown their loyalty; it's a "trust us to look after you because you have chosen us for a major part of your food business".

Another example of Dorothy Lane's reward philosophy was its Anniversary Concert. In 1998, to celebrate its 50th Anniversary, Dorothy Lane rented a stadium in Dayton, and hired the Golden Boys—Frankie Avalon, Fabian, and Bobby Rydell (three popular teen idols of the '50s and '60s)—as entertainment. The company then surprised customers by sending out the first wave of concert invitations to its 500 best customers, allowing them (and a guest) to have the first choice of seats. Invitations to the next level of customers followed. Four thousand of its best customers and their guests enjoyed a free Las Vegas-quality concert, just for being loyal to their food store!

This focus on surprise rewards manifests itself in different ways throughout the year. For example, at least once a quarter Dorothy Lane has an unannounced, extra-special customer sale for a week. (Remember, the company doesn't have weekly newspaper ads, so this is a surprise for its regular customers who shop that week.) It uses the best gondola ends in the store to create excitement. There are special items in each department and different extra special offers can appear on different days. These surprise specials are available to all customers using their *Club DLM* card.

A surprise reward may be as simple as a bouquet of flowers while, at Christmas, it's often an invitation to its very best customers to pick up an elegant, food-related gift next time they are in the store. Over the years these gifts have included a bottle of the finest olive oil and a top quality bread knife; a tall, handsome pepper mill; a full set of upscale, imported chef's knives; and a presentation package including a top-of-the-line cutting board.

SURPRISE POSTCARDS

Every month for the past four years, Dorothy Lane has mailed a variety of postcards to its Key Customers (ie, those who spend, on average, over $25 per week). The postcards are finely targeted to reflect the customer's purchasing behavior. Together with the extreme value offered on the postcard, it aims to trigger upon receipt, a "WOW!" The 50%+ redemption rate reflects the customers' pleasure when they receive individualized offers such as $4 off any seafood purchase (mailed to top seafood customers), free Boston Stoker coffee beans (to heavy coffee drinkers), a free jar of Pine Club Dressing (to heavy salad buyers), $4 off any specialty cheese purchase (to wine buyers), or two dozen free eggs (to most customers). *Club DLM* members never know when they will receive a postcard.

A great feature of postcards is that they are very flexible and low cost. One store's team can decide on an item and a target customer group today and have the postcards in the customers' mailboxes tomorrow.

How can Dorothy Lane afford to have a monthly newsletter with great coupon offers, rewards for its better customers, targeted WOW! postcards, and, at the same time, increase its profits? Simple. The company took the total savings achieved by eliminating its weekly newspaper ad and redirected them away from the mass market towards specific customer markets.

ADDING VALUE

Rewarding regular customers is a mindset at Dorothy Lane. For those who spend $250 in a year, Dorothy Lane, via its Good Neighbor program, donates just under one percent of purchases to a charity of the customer's choice. This is a generous gesture in an industry where the average profits-to-sales ratio is a fraction over one percent. Also, from a business perspective, this approach is a more equitable way of returning profits to the community than writing a check for every organization that knocks on your door seeking a donation.

To add more value to its relationship with customers, Dorothy Lane has developed, over time, an association with more than twenty other Dayton merchants who give a discount—typically ten percent—to any customer presenting her *Club DLM* card when making a purchase. Before becoming an exclusive sector member of the *Club Merchant Program,* each potential merchant is carefully checked by Tom Winter, Dorothy Lane's advertising director, to ensure it is the type of business Dorothy Lane customers would be happy to patronize. Merchant partners run the gamut: from dry cleaners to party stores; from landscaping services to house-cleaning services. Customers can check the current list of Club Merchants at any time on the Dorothy Lane website.

However, developing customer relationships is not done by special prices and rewards alone. It is accomplished by great service and constant customer contact. As Amy Brinkmoeller, director of loyalty marketing, recently told me: "Our *Club DLM* is a great tool with which to reward our customers, but we never allow ourselves to forget that the best continuity program we offer our customers is the great service we provide every day in our stores."

CONSTANTLY LISTENING TO WHAT CUSTOMERS THINK

Every night, at each store, a senior employee calls five customers who shopped that day to get feedback on their experience. Norman Mayne got this idea some years ago from his dentist who called patients who had major dental work that day. Customers' comments are written on special forms with a highlighted section to record any follow-up action required and, then, taken. Upon completion, these forms are circulated to every manager throughout the company.

Every week, each manager and department manager sends a handwritten letter to customers, drawn from the database, thanking them for shopping at Dorothy Lane (and their departments) and inviting them on their next visit to make any suggestions they would like to see implemented.

Comment cards are highly visible for customers to take and complete. In addition, cards seeking comments are randomly put in customers' orders. Even the Internet site has a feedback section.

At each store's exit are *Ask a Question* forms. Customers are invited to pin up any questions they would like to have answered. These questions, along with management's answers, are posted for every customer to read.

For continuous feedback with a long-term perspective, Dorothy Lane has a volunteer customer advisory group. It meets regularly with Norman Mayne over a two-year term to give its thoughts on how the stores are doing, the quality and range of products offered, and to make any suggestions for improvement. In turn, the advisory group is used as a sounding board for new ideas being considered. Several years ago, Norman Mayne was leaving a meeting we had both attended to meet his advisory group in Atlanta. Their first day was spent looking at that city's best food stores in order to learn how Dorothy Lane could be improved; the second day was for personal shopping. Dorothy Lane rewarded participants with airfares, first-class hotel accommodations, and an excellent dining experience. It's no wonder that during the busy

Christmas season these advisory group members are often seen on the shop floor showing new customers where to find items and answering questions about *Club DLM*.

This is a company that is serious about listening to its customers. With the advent of its loyalty card, its customer comprehension has been richly enhanced.

INFORMATION-BASED DIFFERENTIATED MARKETING

Being close to the customer, having the city's most accommodating, friendly, and knowledgeable staff, and offering a clearly differentiated proposition doesn't mean that Dorothy Lane can ignore the intense competition from the three food retail giants that surround it. Rather than trying to compete head-on, however, the company practices classic differentiation strategy. In addition to *straddle pricing* (ie, above a competitor's price for non-cardholders and below it for cardholders) on many items, Dorothy Lane avoids direct price wars with these giants by the frequent use of two tools made possible through its *Club DLM: segmented pricing* and *continuity pricing*.

When these major competitors indulge in their occasional bloodletting price wars, Dorothy Lane chooses to use its own unique weapons as was demonstrated in one recent city-wide milk price war. A gallon of milk generally costs a retailer a little under $2.00 and is sold for just a few cents more. One major competitor, followed quickly by another, dropped its retail price to $0.99. If Dorothy Lane had echoed this move, its profits would have been deeply cut. Instead, it introduced *segmented pricing*. Researching its database, it identified those regular customers who were heavy gallon-milk buyers. Then, with some funding help from its milk supplier, the company mailed postcards offering limited quantities to this vulnerable segment for a mere $0.49 per gallon! A comparable program, aimed at its heavy half-gallon buying segment, followed. The result of this information-based, differentiated marketing response was that Dorothy Lane maintained its company's sales and profits during the giants' summer-long battle!

Even though Dorothy Lane offers many items around the store at lower prices for its *Club DLM* members, its goal is to have long-term relationships with its customers. Thus, the company has a bias towards *continuity pricing.* Its Summer Steak Club is a good example. Instead of having steak specials each week (favoring the occasional customer), it invites *Club DLM* members to enroll in its three-month long Steak Club. Each time a Steak Club member accumulates $50 in spending on steaks, the store sends her a $5 gift certificate. This type of sales-building, opt-in program is highly effective because it appeals only to the customer who regularly buys the items offered. This means that the continuity discount can be deeper than normal because the markdowns are given only to those who signed up; they are not wasted on customers with low or no interest. It also encourages those who opted in to visit the store more frequently to take maximum advantage of the offer. Continuity pricing is an information-based program where all the right players win.

THE CARD IS THE KEY

Once any business is armed with customer information it becomes empowered to act in its customers' interests. To gain that information, Dorothy Lane is always encouraging customers to present their loyalty card when shopping. This is done in various ways, including: two-tier pricing in every aisle (ie, no reduced prices without the card); reminder signs throughout the store; and regular letters to customers in the monthly newsletter, the *Market Report* (like we see in Figure 2) which set out the diverse benefits of always presenting their card.

DEAR CLUB DLM MEMBER

Why Should You Use Your *Club DLM* Card Every Time You Shop?

Our cashiers begin every transaction by asking, "Do you have your *Club DLM* card?" Most of the time, your answer is "yes," but sometimes we hear, "I'm not buying anything on sale, so I don't need to use it." We want to let you know that there are reasons to use your Club DLM card for every transaction.

❖ Your *Club DLM* account is "credited" with every purchase you make, so we are able to send you offers and special promotions via mail. Remember, the cornerstone of Club DLM is that our best customers will be rewarded the most. The more you use your card, the better savings you will receive.

❖ When you sign up for our Good Neighbor Program, your favorite charity will receive up to a 1% rebate on all of your purchases made with your *Club DLM* card. To your charities, small orders can add up quickly. If you haven't signed up already, forms are available near the service booth at both stores.

❖ Every time we scan your *Club DLM* card, you are automatically entered into our monthly raffle. We have given away prizes ranging from DLM gift certificates, to a trip to Club Med in the Bahamas, to a new car!

❖ Don't forget the other benefits of *Club DLM,* including the return of lost keys and the *Club DLM Merchants Program* where you get discounts at numerous other businesses in town.

Club DLM is much more than your way to receive our special in-store prices. It is your key to unlocking great savings and benefits at DLM and other businesses, such as Fraze Pavilion and Motorwerks, Inc.

FIGURE 2: FRONT PAGE OF A RECENT DLM MARKET REPORT

THE BOTTOM LINE

With this focus on rewarding customers, it should be no surprise to learn that customers willingly enroll for their instantly usable, free *Club DLM* card. Nor that Dorothy Lane captures well over 80% of store sales with it, one of the criteria used to identify world-class loyalty leaders.

Business success is never the result of any single factor. Dorothy Lane's continued success, surrounded as it is by some of the industry's toughest competitors, is no exception. *Club DLM* alone is not the reason. However, as we will hear Norman Mayne readily attest, the information it provides has been one of the special gold-tipped arrows in his quiver for building his highly successful business.

A RETAILER'S VIEW

At the end of a recent discussion on loyalty marketing with Norman Mayne, I asked him two questions:

Norman, what's your bottom line on Club DLM?

"Information is power," he responded. "It's power I never had before the Club."

Why, then, don't all retailers have a loyalty card program?

"I don't know. I can't imagine ever running a business blind any more. I just didn't appreciate how blind I was until I saw the data on my customers. Possibly, the main reason why business leaders don't capture and use their customer data is that fearful word ... *change* ... that's scary for some."

BOOMERANG LOYALTY

Feargal Quinn, the founder of Superquinn, learned the essence of customer loyalty and retail success in another industry. In his outstanding book, *Crowning the Customer,* he describes how his summers as a teenager were spent working at his family's holiday camp. Holidaymakers came to this site off the coast of Ireland for one or two weeks. Their stay was paid for up front. Nothing more would be spent; there were no '"extras" to pay at the end of their stay.

Quinn's father had one simple success measure: how many customers signed up to return the following year? This made the role of every family member obvious: make guests happy so that they will want to return again next year. This experience had an impact on the young man. When Feargal Quinn opened his first supermarket in the Dublin area in 1960, the guiding principle he instilled in all employees was— and still is today—*Get the customer to return.* In fact, the *Boomerang Principle* as it has since been dubbed, is now a well-recognized mantra in many parts of the retail world.

As the company's magnetic North Pole, this principle is manifested in many different ways. Superquinn hires friendly people with a ready smile. Employees are taught to recognize and greet customers by name and to make eye contact with them. Customer service desks are highly visible and readily accessible. They are positioned prominently on a front gondola end in each store, so that customers can easily ask questions and express their thoughts. Superquinn truly wants its customers to return!

THE CUSTOMER IS ALL-IMPORTANT

Superquinn is a company where the customer is all-important; where doing everything possible to please them is paramount; where keeping in close contact with them is vital. For these reasons, Feargal Quinn, early in the development of the company, asked a close business friend to take on the chairmanship of the company so that he, Quinn, could spend a significant part of his time on the shop floor listening to and talking with customers.

All top managers are expected to do their own family's shopping at least once a month, either in their own or in a competitor's store, so that they better understand shopping from a customer's perspective. Each is expected to spend at least half a day each week in the stores. To reinforce this mindset, the company has an amusing, albeit serious, lapel pin with the inscription, YCDBSOYA—"You can't do business sitting on your ... armchair!"

Employees at Superquinn are encouraged to have fun. As grocery shopping will always be a chore rather than an enjoyable experience, Feargal Quinn encourages the "fun" element of the business. Celebrations are common. There are frequent interstore contests. Trips to the United States are common prizes for a cross section of employees from the winning stores.

It is a company where other family members are encouraged to join. (Indeed, one store employs six members of the same family.) The company celebrates achievements, anniversaries, birthdays, and even—as I discovered—the national holidays of visitors. One recent July 4th, I was with them for a day of meetings. As I entered the boardroom, the American national anthem was playing and meeting attendees were holding their hands over their hearts. Draped over my chair was a jacket: one half comprised the US flag; the other half was designed with an Irish shamrock! Fun and business mixes well at Superquinn. So much so that many new stores have opened on Feargal Quinn's birthday!

Superquinn is a company where people are important. Employees are called colleagues. As you shop, you see photographs of the farmers who grew the beef that is on sale that week, or those who grew the mushrooms, lettuces, or other vegetable items on display. Further, not just each department, but each section has a photograph of the young man or woman in charge of that particular section. Store managers have an unusually high degree of responsibility and authority. The company's suggestion system readily rewards upward-flowing ideas.

Superquinn believes that customer loyalty is not the game; rather, it is the result of the game. There are many, many facets to the game, as its approach above suggests, all with one common idea—*If we look after our customers they will keep returning and their feeling towards us, their loyalty, will grow deeper.*

WHY A LOYALTY CARD?

Why, then, would Superquinn, a company already obsessed with customers, need to introduce a loyalty card? Frank Murphy, the executive responsible for SuperClub since its inception in 1993 and a member of Superquinn's board of directors, gives four primary reasons:

1. To know better who its customers are

2. To use technology to improve customer service

3. To measure how effective each store is in building customer loyalty

4. To have a vehicle, the card, to more easily offer programs encouraging customers to return

Superquinn is not, however, purely a customer-centric company. It's also a product-centric company. Like Dorothy Lane, it offers an array of unique, specially prepared signature items, which act as customer magnets, drawing customers past competitors' stores to shop at Superquinn.

One signature item is the simple sausage, a part of the Irish heritage. Superquinn set out to produce the very best fresh sausages in Ireland—made in full view of the customers. In fact, these sausages taste so good they regularly win special Irish food awards. Superquinn never worries about its sausages being underpriced by competitors, a traditional retail mindset. Rather, it is concerned should any competitor ever dare to charge a higher price! After all, why wouldn't customers want to pay top price for the very best sausages in Ireland?

Superquinn has built its business over time so that now more than half of its stores' sales comprise fresh items. Freshness is a fetish. Many of the vegetables on display in its stores are picked early that same morning. Tomatoes and bananas are displayed in two piles: "Good for today" and "Good for tomorrow". If any product made fresh that day (such as its sausages or items in its bakery) is not sold at the end of the day, it is not marked down for clearance, a common retail practice, but is donated to charity.

All beef that Superquinn sells is DNA-tested and records are kept of every beef item sold. Several years ago, when Mad Cow Disease caused the sales of beef to plummet in the UK (and at competitors' stores), Superquinn's beef sales rose—because Superquinn, armed with product-specific information, could guarantee the quality of its beef as it knew the origin of each piece sold.

WHERE LISTENING IS AN ART FORM

Superquinn has institutionalized listening to customers. At the core of this listening system is its customer panel. Brochures in each store invite customers to participate:

> Have you got any ideas or opinions about shopping at Superquinn? Have you got any complaints, or any suggestions on how we might improve our service? If you have, you would be more than welcome at our consumer panel, which meets in this store from time to time.
>
> We learn a great deal from these meetings about those little things that can make such a big difference to you, the shopper; things we might miss ourselves because we are so close to the operation! If you can spare the time to help us, please put your name and address on the back of this leaflet and drop it in at the customer service desk.
>
> We'll be in touch next time we are getting together!
> Thanks a lot.

Every fortnight, a different customer panel meets in a different store. Typically, Feargal Quinn and a customer relations specialist, who takes notes, are deliberately heavily outnumbered by a dozen or more customers. This ratio signals to customers that it's their show; that Superquinn wants to listen to them. The meeting is open-ended. Quinn simply asks the panel what they think about all aspects of the company: The outside of the store? The bakery? The range of fish offered? Checkouts? Shopping carts? The way complaints are handled?

His role, he explains, is to sit back and listen. He doesn't try to justify the company's position. He is, as he says, "seeking to hear what he doesn't want to hear." Every comment is recorded, typed, and circulated to each store where colleagues can see what customers are thinking about their company. It also reminds them, of course, that they, likewise, will be critiqued. It's a powerful vehicle to help Superquinn keep in touch with what customers are thinking. Not every suggestion is implemented. Some, as you can imagine, are contradictory. But many excellent features of Superquinn today originally were ideas germinated in one of these customer panel meetings, including:

- ❖ A children's playhouse where children, after being checked in, are looked after by trained supervisors while their parents shop

- ❖ Scissors next to the grape and broccoli displays to enable customers to cut large bunches into smaller sizes more suitable to their needs

- ❖ An umbrella service when it's raining

- ❖ Apples sold by the unit, not by weight. This means, for example, that as the cost of apples vary, they may be offered to customers as six, seven, or eight for £0.99 rather than, say, £1.80 per pound.

Other customers told Quinn that waiting at the checkouts was the most painful part of shopping—so he introduced seats for customers to use while waiting in a checkout line. Customers are also provided with a selection of the day's newspapers to read while waiting! Superquinn is always wanting to find ways to neutralize the painful points of shopping—as we might expect from a company that truly listens to it customers.

Ireland has a population of some 3.5 million people. Among them are ten thousand people who react adversely to wheat-based products. Celiac disease is such a serious problem for those who suffer from it that the Irish government allows sufferers tax relief on any gluten-free products they buy.

After learning of this problem in a customer panel meeting, Quinn decided to something about it. The company introduced attractive shelf signs indicating which products were gluten-free and also identified the items on customers' register tapes. Superquinn then approached the Irish Internal Revenue Service and persuaded it to accept the company's recording of sales of gluten-free products to celiac customers. Superquinn now sends these customers an annual statement of the gluten-free products purchased in its stores. The statements are then submitted by these customers, along with their other tax details, saving them the chore of having to collect, sort, and total all of their register slips.

It's another example of what Feargal Quinn means when he says that we must "use technology to improve customer service." It also shows the power of listening to customers—of jumping across the counter to learn how they view their shopping experience. Of course, such a program would not have been possible without the information power of Superquinn's SuperClub card.

SuperClub

The SuperClub card program, launched in 1993, permeates Superquinn's whole business—and beyond. Its points-based program allows customers to earn points not only in Superquinn's stores but also in 15 other businesses, including the Texaco petrol chain, a national sporting goods retailer, a home improvement chain, and a hotel group.

Each partner offers points based upon the amount the cardholder spends. At Superquinn, customers earn points not only on their total spending but also when they buy designated items around the store. Selected customers are also offered points as a reward when certain frequency or spending thresholds are met.

Twice a year, SuperClub issues an attractive catalog containing over 700 items redeemable for points. The range of items offered is diverse. Some of the product categories featured in its catalog include:

- Audiovisual
- Bathroom
- Bedroom
- Cameras
- Cutlery
- Gardening Tools
- Giftware
- Golf
- Kitchen Appliances
- Nursery Gifts
- Telephones
- Toys
- Vacuum Cleaners
- Watches

The catalog also features a wide selection of extremely attractive travel offers. Along with the redemption of a specified number of SuperClub points, a member can buy special low-priced airfares to most parts of the world, both near and far. Over a hundred diverse destinations are listed, including Manchester, Moscow, and Madrid; Oslo, Orlando, and Ontario; Beijing, Boston, and Bangkok.

Another special section offers a variety of partners' gift certificates available in exchange for varying amounts of points. For example, 800 points for a £5 gift certificate at Superquinn; 900 points for a £5 gift certificate at a major book chain; 2,000 points for £20 gift certificate at a major hotel chain.

And if that isn't enough, any customer who would like an item that isn't in the catalog can call the SuperClub hotline where she can ask for a quote, in points, for the item. If the customer accepts the quote, the item will be ordered. In other words, the customer decides when, where, and how points are used! A customer even has the choice of passing them on to a friend or donating them to a charity or other worthy cause.

Customer pleasing knows few boundaries at Superquinn. As Eamonn Quinn, Superquinn's marketing director and deputy chairman, has pointed out, "We must always keep in mind that points are there to reward the customer for shopping at Superquinn."

FEEDBACK IS THE BREAKFAST OF CHAMPIONS

Superquinn is a very open, yet very accountable company. Every Thursday morning, members of the senior management team from its Support Center visit each store. They go from department to department, sharing with all employees how the previous week's trading and customer results compare with the week's target (flexed for the trading pattern of that week) and with peer performances at both department and store levels within the company. This means that all employees receive both a horizontal and vertical perspective of their department: sales, profits, and customer information.

Ever since it began gathering customer information the company has recognized its importance. For example, it has changed its store manager bonus program from being based solely on the store's profits to a combination of the store's profits and changes in the Best Customer count. This was a result of Superquinn finding that changes in a store's Best Customer numbers directly reflected changes in the basic loyalty elements—service, cleanliness, in-stock conditions, etc—of that store.

USING CUSTOMER INFORMATION

Superquinn is not only a company that is warm and friendly but is also smart and strategic. This is demonstrated by its recent development of TUSA, a 50:50 joint venture with one of Ireland's banks. In this venture, Superquinn brings to the banking industry the supermarket principles of high volume, low costs, extra-friendly service, and extreme convenience (deposits and withdrawals can be made at checkouts at any time the stores are open). This development is a natural outcome of a company that knows its customers. Based upon its customers' spending profiles, Superquinn can quickly identify which are most likely to be interested in a banking relationship when they visit one of their stores. Having already experienced Superquinn's superior care and service, its customers are, of course, more likely to move their banking relationships to a company where Superquinn is a principal shareholder.

Further, to build the synergy between both operations, TUSA debit or credit card holders—who automatically become SuperClub cardholders—earn double points when using their card at Superquinn. TUSA is another example of using technology to improve customer service.

Yet another example is Superquinn's *Save Your Change* program that allows customers to leave their change behind after shopping and have it saved, with their SuperClub card number being their account number. Some customers regularly set aside cash each week to help budget for Christmas and family events. Savings can be easily withdrawn. Just scan your card and enter your PIN number at one of the in-store kiosks (in the same way as one does at an ATM).

Superquinn uses its rich insight into customers in various other ways as well. For example, Damien Carolan, Superquinn's top merchandise executive, now checks which Best Customers, if any, are buying a particular product before a decision is made to delete or replace it with another product.

The company has embraced customer information because of its power to help it understand the customer better and, through that understanding, make it a better retailer. Customer information helps the company:

- ❖ Measure its effectiveness in building loyalty
- ❖ Measure its appeal in the marketplace (including word-of-mouth recommendations) by monitoring the rate of new customer additions
- ❖ Detect early any adverse below-the-surface changes in store or company trends by noting changes in weekly customer indicators
- ❖ Target different customer segments cost-effectively
- ❖ Evaluate the attractiveness of each department's weekly features by measuring how many households shopped in each department

THE BOTTOM LINE

Superquinn is, in my experience, one of the world's best retailers. It is customer-centric, with an overriding goal of getting its customers to return. Its focus is reinforced by the inclusion of Best Customer measures as a key component of its bonus program. The company seeks to use technology to improve the customer experience. Management listens to and communicates with customers and colleagues alike. Sales, profits, and customer performance results are shared with all employees. Superquinn is a wonderful example of how a company can have fun and be highly successful at the same time.

The company's mission statement—*To be a world-class team renowned for excellence in fresh food and customer service*—reflects both its vision and its customers' experience.

A RETAILER'S VIEW

The same two questions I asked Norman Mayne were also posed to Feargal Quinn:

Feargal, what's your bottom line on SuperClub?

"I see three primary benefits:

1. It allows us to measure our most valuable asset, our customers.

2. It allows us to develop better, stronger interpersonal relationships with customers.

3. It allows us to identify, recognize, and thank our best customers."

Why, then, don't all retailers have a loyalty card program?

"The cost. Loyalty card programs have a cost. Some companies see this cost as much greater than the benefit derived. Some companies either don't understand or don't appreciate the value of the customer information generated. Others have introduced very costly programs and don't feel the information they get provides enough return in exchange. Some think that a loyalty program is like the old Green Shield trading stamp program—but they forget one major fact: trading stamp programs never provided customer information to improve their business."

CUSTOMER CHURN & BURN

Chapter **2**

One piece of data has exploded many a balloon of opinion.
... Richard Sloma

We are standing in the middle of our own acres of diamonds.
... Russell Conwell

Mass marketers have never known the actual ebb and flow of their customers. Marketing decisions were based on assumptions about customer behavior with billions of dollars being spent in the process. Weekly advertisements were placed in newspapers with clockwork regularity in the belief that they would attract new customers and that existing customers would be enticed to return. But no one ever knew how valid these passionately held assumptions were—until now. Today, with data from our loyalty card programs, we can track activity and discover our customers' diverse shopping patterns. We can measure the changes in their behavior as we vary the different elements of our business proposition. At long last, we can put the feet of our assumptions to the fire of measurement.

WHAT THIS CHAPTER WILL SHOW YOU

The purpose of this chapter is to show you what goes on below the surface of our businesses. Using one retailer's actual results as an example, you will see that:

1. There is a great deal of customer turbulence

2. There is a natural decline in customer spending

3. Few New Customers soon become Best Customers

4. The loss rate of New Customers is very high

5. The loss rate of Reactivated Customers is very high

I. THERE IS A GREAT DEAL OF CUSTOMER TURBULENCE

Recently, a company concerned about its slowing sales growth invited us to provide it with an independent review of its performance. The results of this very strong food chain, used throughout the chapter, are representative of the industry except that, in many cases, they are better than those of the average chain. To disguise the company we will call it Blake Stores and convert its base quarter results to 10,000 customers per store.

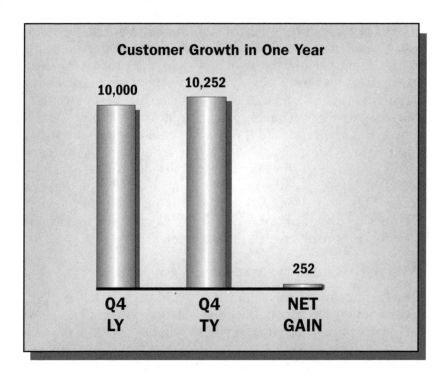

FIGURE 3: CUSTOMER GROWTH IN ONE YEAR

As customers are the lifeblood of every business, we began our analysis with Blake's year-to-year change in customer numbers. We found that the number of active customers per store this year ("TY") had increased by 2.5% over last year ("LY") (Figure 3). In these competitive times, that was a very good increase.

We then went below the surface (see Figure 4) to understand what ebb and flow of customers had occurred to produce this gain. That's where we saw the heavy customer turbulence.

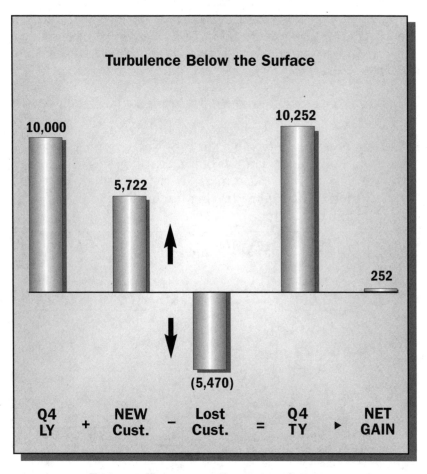

FIGURE 4: TURBULENCE BELOW THE SURFACE

During the year, the average Blake store had enjoyed a New Customer inflow of 57.2%. Unfortunately, this strong inflow was offset by a comparably strong outflow of 54.7%.

If we include in the customer base the New Customers acquired during the year, we can say that the 5,470-customer outflow was at a 34.8% rate.

Blake had certainly been successful in gaining new customers—but was letting a large number of them slip through its fingers again. To have a customer inflow of over 50% of one's base—customers who went to the effort of applying for a loyalty card—and yet end up a year later with a net increase of customers of just 2.5%, highlights the turbulent nature of our marketplace. *Customers are flowing into our store in large numbers but are flowing out again just as freely.*

2. THERE IS A NATURAL DECLINE IN CUSTOMER SPENDING

Another way of showing the inflow and outflow of customers is presented in Figure 5. Not only does it show the inflow and outflow totals but it also allows us to compare the composition of customers in the fourth quarter last year (which is the same as saying the beginning of this year) and the fourth quarter of this year.

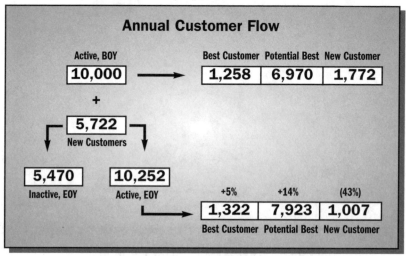

FIGURE 5: CUSTOMER FLOW AT BLAKE STORES

We see, for example, that the average Blake store increased its Best Customers (those spending over $50 week) by 5% from year-end last year to year-end this year. This raises the question: What was the source of those Best Customers? How many came from each of the three segments—Best, Potential Best and New—from last year and how many came from the inflow of New Customers this year?

The analysis at Blake revealed what we see at other companies: even though there is a lot of movement of customers among segments during the year, both up and down, *the natural tendency for members of every customer segment is to decrease their spending over time.* This is illustrated in Figures 6-8.

From the final quarter of last year to that of this year, we found that 22% of this company's Best Customers had dropped to a lower spending level and 3% had defected. In other words, 25% of its Best Customers in the fourth quarter of last year had dropped to a lower level in the fourth quarter this year (Figure 6).

Blake Stores had a similar experience with its Potential Best Customers. Even though 4% of them moved up to become Best Customers from last year to this year, another 23% had defected (Figure 7). Again, the natural tendency was more downwards (in this case to zero) than upwards.

This natural spending decline also occurs in the more narrowly defined segments. For example, we saw it among the Opals ($25-$50 per week), who comprise the top half of the Potential Best Customers. This group is important because it is populated by the prime prospects for our Best Customer segment.

We found that 19% of last year's Opals did, indeed, increase their spending to become Best Customers this year (Figure 8). Unfortunately, this was more than offset by another 32% of them who dropped their weekly spending to less than $25 (Pearls) and a further 6% who defected. In other words, 19% of this pivotal segment had increased their spending— while 38% had decreased theirs.

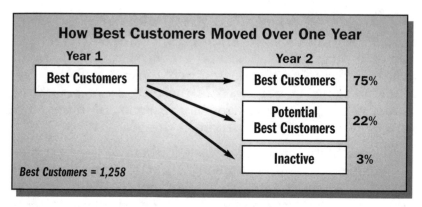

FIGURE 6: BEST CUSTOMERS ONE YEAR LATER

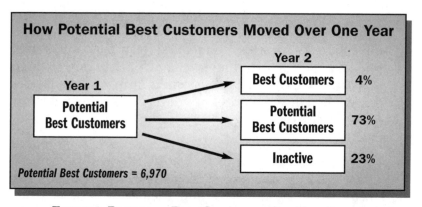

FIGURE 7: POTENTIAL BEST CUSTOMERS ONE YEAR LATER

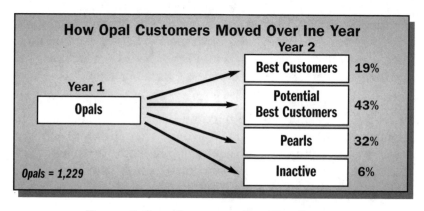

FIGURE 8: OPAL CUSTOMERS ONE YEAR LATER

3. FEW NEW CUSTOMERS SOON BECOME BEST CUSTOMERS

Using the same analysis as used in Figures 6-8, we found another remarkable statistic—only 1% of last year's New Customers had gravitated to Best Customer status one year later (Figure 9), illustrating that *few New Customers soon become Best Customers.*

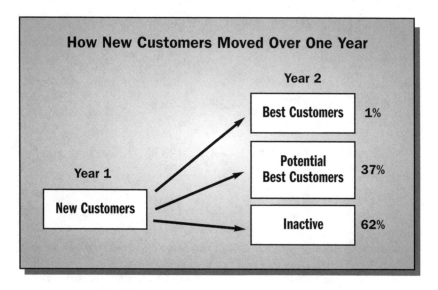

How New Customers Moved Over One Year

Year 2

Best Customers — 1%

Potential Best Customers — 37%

Year 1

New Customers

Inactive — 62%

FIGURE 9: NEW CUSTOMERS ONE YEAR LATER

The lesson from this finding—again, a common one among retailers—is that New Customers are definitely not a fertile area for growing Best Customer numbers in the short term. The primary candidates for Best Customers are already with us. They are members of our Potential Best Customers group.

4. THE LOSS RATE OF NEW CUSTOMERS IS VERY HIGH

Another surprising statistic is revealed in Figure 9. In the fourth quarter of this year, Blake had lost 62% of those customers who were new to the company 12 months earlier. Obviously, such a loss was an important factor in Blake's total customer outflow during the year.

In addition, when we looked at the behavior of New Customers in the first three quarters of this year, we also learned that they don't wait a year before leaving. New Customers start defecting almost immediately after their first visit.

New (First Time) in...	Qtr.1	Qtr.2	Qtr.3	Total
First Time in Qtr.	767	732	657	2,156
Still Active in Qtr. 4	325	301	327	953
Inactive in Qtr. 4	(442)	(431)	(330)	(1,203)
Outflow Rate	(58)%	(59)%	(50)%	(56)%

TABLE 10: FIRST TIME NEW CUSTOMERS IN QUARTERS 1-3 THIS YEAR

There was an average outflow rate of 56% of New Customers who shopped for the first time in the first nine months this year in the fourth quarter (Table 10). Even of those who shopped for the first time in the third quarter, 50% did not return to shop in the fourth quarter! *The loss rate of New Customers is, indeed, very high.*

A word of caution is needed here, however. Chains that are smaller than Blake Stores will have higher New Customer outflow rates while larger chains will experience lower outflow rates. The reason is simple. The more stores a chain has, the more opportunities there are for a customer to shop in one of them, even if the customer moves. Thus, a nationwide chain like Kroger will have a lower customer outflow rate than a two-unit operation like Dorothy Lane.

5. THE LOSS RATE OF REACTIVATED CUSTOMERS IS VERY HIGH

Reactivated Customers are those customers who return to shop after having defected. In the case of food retailers, this means after being inactive for at least one full quarter.

Currently, most retailers have no idea of either the magnitude or behavior of their Reactivated Customers. They should, because Reactivated Customers don't remain active very long—they flip back to an inactive status at a very high rate.

New (Reactivated) in...	Qtr.1	Qtr.2	Qtr.3	Total
Reactivated in Qtr.	1,276	844	439	2,559
Still Active in Qtr. 4	576	302	168	1,046
Inactive in Qtr. 4	(700)	(542)	(271)	(1,513)
Outflow Rate	(55)%	(64)%	(62)%	(59)%

TABLE 11: REACTIVATED CUSTOMERS IN QUARTERS 1-3 THIS YEAR

At Blake Stores, the outflow of Reactivated Customers was comparable to that of New Customers. In the fourth quarter of this year, 59% of those who had reactivated their relationship sometime in the first nine months were inactive again (Table 11). *It's a loss rate that is both very high and puzzling.*

. This high loss of Reactivated Customers has always surprised me. These are customers who have shopped with us previously and have chosen, after an absence, to return and shop again. But then, almost immediately, many of them stop shopping yet again. The high outflow rate means, presumably, that we stopped satisfying these customers last year for some reason and, when they returned, we still didn't satisfy them enough to make them want to shop with us again on a regular basis.

The high churn of both Reactivated and "First Time" New Customers is a riddle yet to be solved. Fortunately, using customer information, retailers are beginning to reduce their churn rates, but there is still a huge opportunity for improvement.

The reader should note that Reactivated and First Time New Customers have similar characteristics. For this reason, they are often aggregated and included under the common heading of New Customers for analysis purposes.

CUSTOMER FLOW ANALYSIS

The methodology used in the preceding analysis is called Customer Flow analysis. Public companies include a Funds Flow statement in their Annual Reports to show how their cash "flowed" during the year: what cash they began the year with, where it came from, what it was spent on, and then how much was left at year's end. Customer Flow analysis performs a similar function with customers.

As you think about the preceding analysis, keep in mind that every business has two primary customer goals:

1. To increase the number of active customers per store over the previous year, and

2. To improve the quality of its customer base, ie, to increase the share of higher-spending, higher-profit customers.

Customer Flow analysis allows us to measure how effective we are in accomplishing these two goals. It also allows us to look below the surface of these headline numbers and see the effect of customer churn. In particular, we can see how many inactive customers reactivate (ie, start shopping again), how many customers start shopping with us for the first time, and how much outflow we experience with both of these groups—as well as with those customers who were shopping with us at the beginning of the year. Only when we know these specifics can we introduce appropriate programs to strengthen our net customer flow.

CUSTOMER QUALITY

The first primary customer goal has already been well addressed. We will now turn to the second goal. Using Blake Stores again as an example, we will examine whether it improved the quality of its customer base from year to year.

As seen in Table 12, we compared the customer mix in the final quarters of both years. The results were very positive. Blake had not only increased its active customer base by 2.5% but had also skewed its customer mix more towards its higher spenders.

Both the number of Best Customers (those spending over $50 per week) and Potential Best Customers (under $50 per week) had improved by 5.1% and 13.7%, respectively (col. d). The disappointment was that the number of New Customers in the quarter was down from the previous year. (Fortunately, Blake, once aware of the problem, was easily able to remedy that.)

(a)	(b)	(c)	(d)	(e)	(f)
Customer Segment	**LY Total**	**TY Total**	**TY/LY Change**	**LY %Total**	**TY %Total**
1. Best Customers	1,258	1,322	5.1%	12.6%	12.9%
2. Potential BC's	6,970	7,923	13.7%	69.7%	77.3%
3. New Customers	1,772	1,007	(43.2)%	17.7%	9.8%
4. TOTAL	**10,000**	**10,252**	**2.5%**	**100.0%**	**100.0%**

TABLE 12: YEAR-TO-YEAR CUSTOMER MIX COMPARISON

Qualitatively, the most important year-to-year change was the 5.1% increase of its Best Customers—which was twice the 2.5% overall customer growth rate. An increase in Best Customers is a positive sign because it usually means that the company has improved its ability to satisfy its higher-profit high-spending customers. It also suggests continued strong sales in the coming months because this segment has a very low defection rate, as was seen in Figure 6.

Our assessment was that if Blake could continue to build those programs that were growing its Best Customers, and introduce programs that would more effectively attract and hold New Customers, the company would be back on its previous upward trajectory.

This exercise was another reminder to me of the power of customer information. How can any business ever hope to increase the number and quality of its customers if it doesn't have a yardstick against which to measure its progress?

BALANCING THE UPS AND DOWNS

One question sometimes asked is: Given the natural spending decline of customers across all sectors and the low conversion rate of New to Best Customers, how then do we increase the number of Best Customers?

The answer is to ensure that our total marketing efforts encourage enough Potential Best Customers to step up their spending to Best Customer status to offset the number of Best Customers dropping out of that segment.

When constructing the various spending breakpoints, retailers usually plan for Best Customers to comprise 12% to 25% of total customers. This means that the number of Potential Best Customers is always a significantly higher number than that of Best Customers. It follows that a large percentage fall-off of Best Customers can be offset by a much smaller percentage of upgrading Potential Best Customers.

To illustrate, Blake had 1,258 Best Customers and 6,970 Potential Best Customers in its base quarter (Figure 5). One year later, 282 Best Customers—a significant 22% of them—had moved down to the lower spending level (Figure 6). This drop would be offset by just 4% of the Potential Best Customer group upgrading (282/6,970 = 4%).

THE LOSS PATTERN OF CUSTOMERS

We have found that the highest spending customers always have the lowest defection rate. As customer spending falls, defection rates rise, with new customers having the highest defection rate. A summary of customer defections at Blake demonstrates this.

	(a)	(b)	(c)	(d)=(c-b)	(e)=(d/b)
		Active		**Inactive in Q4 TY**	
		Q4 LY	**Q4 TY**	**Q4 TY**	**%**
	Customers in Q4 LY				
1	Best Customers	1,258	1,221	(37)	(3)%
2	Potential Best Customers	6,970	5,346	(1,624)	(23)%
3	New in Q4 LY	1,772	679	(1,093)	(62)%
4	**Total Customers Q4 LY**	**10,000**	7,246	(2,754)	(28)%
5	**add New This Year...**				
6	New in Q1, Q2, Q3 TY	4,715	1,999	(2,716)	(58)%
7	= Sub-Total	14,715	9,245	(5,470)	(37)%
8	+ New in Q4 TY	1,007	1,007		
9	**=Total**	**15,722**	**10,252**		

TABLE 13: CUSTOMER LOSS SUMMARY BY SEGMENT

At Blake Stores, three percent (3%) of its Best Customers were inactive one year later, compared to 23% of its Potential Best Customers, and 62% of its New Customers (Table 13, col. e). In addition, 58% of New Customers in the first three quarters of this year did not reappear in the fourth quarter (row 6, col. e).

THE BOTTOM LINE

Customers are not in abundance. They flow into our stores in large numbers and then too many, too readily, flow out again. Both our Reactivated and First Time New Customers are fickle, and only a few move quickly to Best Customer status.

To build a successful business, it's essential that we track our customer flows from year to year, understand their causes, and then build appropriate fences to keep our customers inside. Not only must we keep them inside, we must also focus on growing their spending levels, pushing against the tide of the natural decline in customer spending. Customer Flow analysis is a critical tool that helps us identify these problems and measure our success.

The churn and burn of customers quantified in this chapter is a serious reminder that the foundations of our customers' loyalty are forever being eaten away by the termites of competition, ignorance, inertia, and weak retail differentiation. These business pillars demand constant strengthening if we hope to successfully withstand and weather the ravages of time.

FROM DECILES TO THRESHOLDS

Chapter **3**

Too many reports suffer from the APK—Anxious Parade of Knowledge—syndrome. This is usually the case when the presenter is more concerned with what's been put into the chart than what the audience gets out of it.

... Gene Zelazny, *Say It With Charts*

Retailers who measure customer activity have drawn from both direct marketing and retail management practices. Decades of experience of direct marketers, especially those selling by catalog, have shown us how to measure success from a customer-centric perspective.

Direct marketers taught us the value of breaking customers into equal-sizes groups, each with their own set of unique behavior characteristics. The breakdown is into ten equal groups, or deciles. In this chapter, we will see how some retailers have taken this concept and adapted it for the practicalities of their industry.

Direct marketers also taught us how to optimize results when making targeted offers, again using the concept of equal-size groups. This is achieved by using an intermixing of three factors: *Recency,* or how long ago a customer last shopped; *Frequency*, or how frequently she shopped in a recent period (eg, the last six months); and *Monetary Value* or *Spending* (ie, how much she spent in that period). This is commonly called the RFM or RFS methodology, and will be discussed in Chapter 10.

49

It's often said that better measurement leads to better results. For example, marathon runners are able to see where they need improvement through accurate time measurements at various points of their 26.2-mile course. Runners in major marathons today attach what's called a v-chip to one of their shoelaces. This tiny chip triggers a timing device to record their exact starting, intermediate, and finishing times as they cross special mats stretched across the road along the course. By knowing their times along different parts of the race, these athletes are helped in their training and preparations for later marathons.

In like manner, using previously unknown information about customers helps us improve our overall performance.

DECILE REPORTS

As mentioned, a key report prepared by a direct marketer is the decile report. It is based on a ranking of customers, from highest to lowest spender, divided into ten equal customer groups.

Retailers have had to modify this report when adopting it for their use. They found that if they wanted their employees to be accountable for results, employees had to be provided with a stable set of measurements enabling them to compare their performance from period to period. Retailers found that although deciles are wonderful for targeted mailings, a primary use by direct marketers, they lack the stable base required for interperiod comparisons.

Table 14 shows one large retailer's quarterly Decile Report, expressed per 10,000 customer households. The households total is broken into ten equal groups of 1,000 each. In each row, we see the behavior characteristics of that particular decile.

For example, the top 10% of customers, in decile 10, "visited" (ie, bought something from us) an average of 2.42 times per week in the quarter and spent an average of $34.90 on each visit, or $84.46 per week (2.42 x $34.90 = $84.46). This top decile accounted for 26.9% of all cardholder visits and 37.5% of their sales.

	(a)	(b)	(c)	(d)	(e)	(f)	(g)	(h)	(i)
Deciles	Households	Visits per week	Spend per visit	Spend per week	Households	Total visits in Qtr.	Cum % (Visits)	Tot. spent in Qtr.	Cum % (Spent)
Dec #	**HH #**	**VPW #**	**SPV $**	**SPW $**	**HHs %**	**Visits %**	**Cum %**	**Spend %**	**Cum %**
10	1,000	2.42	34.90	84.46	10.0	26.9	26.9	37.5	37.5
9	1,000	1.71	27.60	47.20	10.0	19.0	45.9	20.9	58.4
8	1,000	1.35	23.64	31.91	10.0	15.0	60.9	14.2	72.6
7	1,000	1.05	21.14	22.20	10.0	11.7	72.6	9.9	82.5
6	1,000	0.80	19.02	15.22	10.0	8.9	81.5	6.8	89.3
5	1,000	0.61	17.20	10.49	10.0	6.8	88.3	4.7	94.0
4	1,000	0.44	15.65	6.89	10.0	4.9	93.2	3.1	97.1
3	1,000	0.30	12.96	3.89	10.0	3.3	96.5	1.7	98.8
2	1,000	0.20	10.52	2.10	10.0	2.2	98.7	0.9	99.7
1	1,000	0.12	6.10	0.73	10.0	1.3	100.0	0.3	100.0
Total	10,000	0.90	25.00	22.50	100.0	100.0		100.0	

TABLE 14: DECILE REPORT

The behavior of these top customers contrasts vividly with the more typical customer as seen in decile 5, who visited the chain only 0.61 times per week during the quarter, whose weekly spending averaged $10.49, and whose purchases accounted for 4.7% of cardholder sales.

A comparison with a customer in the bottom decile further illustrates this point, where visits averaged only 0.12 times and spending $0.73 per week. Spending by customers in Decile 1 accounted for only 0.3% of cardholder sales.

Comparing the spending per week of a customer in decile 10 with customers in deciles 5 and 1, we see that during this quarter, a decile 10 customer spent, on average, over eight times that of a decile 5 customer and a massive 116 times that of a decile 1 customer.

For food retailers, one rule of thumb is that the top decile (the top 10% of customers) accounts for close to 40% of sales, the top two deciles (the top 20%, or top quintile) account for close to 60% of sales, and the top three deciles (top 30%) account for close to 75% of sales. (This is seen in the first three rows of col. i.) Given this, it's worth noting that some world-class loyalty practitioners, with a focused effort, have been able to outperform these rules of thumb and raise the share of sales of their top 20% and 30% of customers' to over 60% and 75% sales, respectively!

The Decile Report in Table 14 clearly demonstrates that *all customers are not equal,* the underlying principle of differentiated marketing—making different offers to different customers based upon their contribution to the business. The report readily helps us to identify which customers are providing the bulk of our business.

A Decile Report is an excellent way to understand the diversity of our customer base, but it is difficult to use as an internal management tool because it tracks a moving target. Every day, the number of members in each decile changes as the total number of customers changes due to the addition of new customers and the deletion of inactive customers from our database.

With such an ever-changing base, it would be difficult for management to ask an executive to be responsible for the company's top customers (say, the top two deciles) and another for the high potentials (say, the next two deciles). Further, as the numbers in each decile change so do its behavior metrics, adding to the difficulty of accountability.

THRESHOLD REPORTS

As the name suggests, a Threshold Report classifies customers based on fixed spending thresholds, such as those customers who spend $100 or more per week or those who spend less than $25 per week. It uses the same data as a decile report but presents it differently.

To prepare this report, customers who shopped in the quarter are initially sorted into three groups:

1. Those who shopped for the first time in the quarter. These are our First Time New Customers.

2. Those who were active both in the quarter and the preceding quarter. These are our Pre-Existing Active Customers (PEAs).

3. Those who have been inactive (ie, they did not shop in the preceding quarter and possibly other prior quarters) but returned to shop this quarter. These are our Reactivated Customers.

Next, we classify our Pre-Existing Active Customers (PEAs) according to how much they spent in the quarter. In US food retailing, as seen in Table 15, the most common sort breakpoints are $100, $50, and $25 per week. The easy-to-remember DROP'N acronym (Diamonds, Rubies, Opals, Pearls, and New) describes these spending classifications. Note that Reactivated Customers are included with First Time New Customers because of similar characteristics, as we saw in the previous chapter.

	Customer Classification	Threshold Breakpoints	
		Spent in 13-week Qtr.	Avg. Spend Per Week
D	Diamonds	> $1,300	> $100
R	Rubies	$650 - 1,300	$50 - 100
O	Opals	$325 - 649	$25 - 49.99
P	Pearls	< $325	< $25
N	New		

TABLE 15: DROP'N THRESHOLD CUSTOMER CLASSIFICATION

Some additional comments are appropriate:

❖ Both threshold breakpoints and the review period (eg, quarters) may vary depending on your type of business.

❖ New customers are put into a separate category because the average new customer shops for only half of the quarter (as new ones are joining each week during the whole quarter) and they have a high dropout rate. Thus, they would unfairly distort the results of the other segments if included with them.

❖ New customers stay in the New Customer segment only during their initial quarter. Thereafter, they are classified according to their quarterly spending.

❖ An active customer is defined as anyone who shops ("visits") at least once in the quarter, regardless of the amount spent.

(A) Spending Thresholds (DROP'N)

GROUP	Households	Visits per week	Spend per visit	Spend per week	Households	Total visits in Qtr.	Cum % (Visits)	Tot. spent in Qtr.	Cum % (Spent)
Customer Type	HHs #	VPW #	SPV $	SPW $	HHs %	Visits %	Cum %	Spend %	Cum %
Diamonds	198	3.10	40.34	125.05	2.0	6.8	6.8	11.1	11.1
Rubies	1,121	2.15	31.94	68.67	11.2	26.8	33.6	34.0	45.0
Opals	1,766	1.41	24.60	34.69	17.7	27.7	61.3	28.1	73.1
Pearls	6,166	0.52	16.55	8.61	61.7	35.7	96.9	23.6	96.7
New	749	0.37	26.20	9.69	7.5	3.1	100.0	3.3	100.0
Total	10,000	0.90	25.00	22.50	100.0	100.0		100.0	

Diamonds >$100 per week; Rubies $50-100; Opals $25-49.99; Pearls < $25 per week

(B) Spending Thresholds (<u>Abbreviated</u> DROP'N)

Customer Type	HHs #	VPW #	SPV $	SPW $	HHs %	Visits %	Cum %	Spend %	Cum %
Best	1,319	2.29	33.50	76.80	13.2	33.6	33.6	45.0	45.0
Potential Best	7,932	0.72	20.41	14.67	79.3	63.3	96.9	51.7	96.7
PEA's	9,251	0.94	24.95	23.53	92.5	96.9	96.9	96.7	96.7
New	749	0.37	26.57	9.83	7.5	3.1	100.0	3.3	100.0
Total	10,000	0.90	25.00	22.50	100.0	100.0		100.0	

Best $50+ per week; Potential Best < $50 per week; PEA's = Pre-Existing Actives

TABLE 16: THRESHOLD REPORTS

Table 16 comprises two threshold reports, the bottom report (B) being an abbreviated version of the top report (A). In the top report, we see the five classes of customers, DROP'N. The behavior characteristics listed in the columns of the report are the same as those in the decile report, Table 14. Additionally, the bottom line totals in the threshold reports are the same as those in the decile report as they are simply a different expression of the same data.

The abbreviated threshold report compresses the four Pre-Existing Active Customer categories (PEAs) into two: those customers spending $50 or more per week (the Diamonds and Rubies), and those under that level (the Opals and Pearls). Those above $50 per week are called Best Customers (BCs). They typically comprise 12% to 25% of a company's customers and 40% to 65% of its sales. The other customers, those spending less than $50 per week, we optimistically call our Potential Best Customers (PBCs).

Best Customers

The abbreviated Threshold Report gets to the essence of our business. It identifies our Best Customers — the best indicator of past and likely future performance that we have of our business. A decline in their numbers usually indicates that parts of our current offering (service, friendliness, assortment, price, and cleanliness) are disappointing our core customer constituency and need immediate investigation and correction.

Because of the importance of this single measure — the number of Best Customers per store — some of the world's best loyalty retailers now incorporate it into their on-going bonus programs. Such companies understand that Best Customers are their primary customers who spend a lot and generate some of the company's highest gross profit percentages. Therefore, to the degree that a company can increase their number, it will enjoy increased sales and profits.

Internally, one major user of this breakdown into Best and Potential Best Customers is the category manager. Category managers track their category's performance on a quarterly basis and measure how effective they have been in marketing to their company's Best Customers. As Best Customers are those who spend the bulk of their dollars with these companies, it's critical to understand how many of them are buying from each category during each quarter. And of those who do, to know how much are they spending in the category.

Further, the category managers measure the retention rate of these customers, compared to the overall company's retention rate of Best Customers. In addition, they benchmark their Best Customer category performance against nationwide industry performance metrics, tracked in various household panels by companies such as ACNielsen and IRI, as they are all measuring customers with similar annual spending levels.

POTENTIAL BEST CUSTOMERS

Potential Best Customers (PBCs) are the Opals and Pearls. Opals, who spend $25-49.99 per week, are usually shoppers who split their shopping between our competitors and us although some, of course, may be people who live alone and are not heavy spenders.

Pearls, who spend less than $25 per week, are occasional customers. They either buy most of our offering elsewhere or they have little need for our selection. Targeted offers to this group generally elicit a very poor response. However, as drop-in, infrequent shoppers, their individual transactions can be quite profitable.

Our first challenge with customers in the PBC group is to encourage them to move up to the Best Customer group. Our second challenge is to ensure that, over time, they are not reducing their spending with us in favor of our competitors.

In summary, the advantages of a Threshold Report are:

❖ It is easy to understand. Eyes often glaze over when we try to explain deciles. But talk of customers who spend over $100 per week, or between $50 and $100 per week, and the comprehension is obvious.

❖ It has fixed spending levels. A threshold report provides a stable measurement base from quarter to quarter, so it's easy to see where customer gains and losses are occurring by spending level.

❖ It is excellent for goals and accountability. For example, a goal of increasing by 3% the number of customers spending over $50 per week is easy to set, and later, easy to measure.

MEANINGFUL MEASUREMENTS

The examples we have discussed in this chapter use quarterly reporting periods. The same methodology, of course, can be used for periods of any length: a week, month, half or full year. The correct period length depends on the nature of your business, the purpose of your analysis, and your customer purchase frequency. As loyalty author Donald Libey reminds us, frequency can range from one day (newspapers) to 100 years (bridge replacements).

In most forms of retailing, we have found that customer performance reports that coincide with our fiscal quarters are preferable because this simplifies the subsequent step of linking customer data to our financial data. However, that should not deter a company from preparing rolling quarter customer reports every month alongside the regular financial reports.

A common characteristic of customer reports is the expression of customer results on an average weekly basis, rather than as totals per month or quarter. This is done to permit easy comparisons, both between fiscal quarters of different lengths and between different regions and companies.

When establishing your customer database one issue to resolve is whether customer activity should be analyzed on a cardholder or household basis. The latter is an approach where all cardholders with the same name living at the same address are linked and treated as one unit for evaluation and marketing purposes. The right approach for you will depend upon what you sell and how you intend to use the data.

Boots The Chemists, for example, tracks behavior by individual customer because it has found that the buying behavior of members of the same household can be quite different—a teenage daughter often buys different soaps and fragrances than her mother. Given that Boots targets cardholders with customer specific offers at its in-store kiosks, it's critical that the appropriate product offer is made to each individual customer.

The same applies to book retailers with loyalty card programs such as Books-A-Million and Barnes & Noble. Reading preferences and, therefore, purchase habits within the same household do vary enormously.

On the other hand, most food retailers find that house-holding their customer data is more appropriate. Whether the husband, wife, or a young adult in the family is buying food, cleaning items, etc, it usually is for the common use of the household. Thus, when food retailers make targeted offers they are addressed to "the Jones Household".

CUSTOMER ACCOUNTING

Traditional retailers use their departmental sales and gross profits as key management tools. With customer data we can now prepare similar management reports, breaking the business into customer groups rather than product groups, as seen in Table 17. In this simple example, we see that the company's average weekly sales per store for the 4-week period was $200,000.

Average Per Week   **Department Gross Profit Account**   *Period: 4 Weeks*

Department Results						
Department	**Grocery**	**Meat**	**Produce**	**Deli/Bky.**	**Gn. Merch.**	**Total**
Sales	126,600	31,200	17,400	11,000	13,800	200,000
Gross Profit	33,042	8,362	5,533	4,292	2,995	54,224
Gross Profit %	26.1%	26.8%	31.8%	39.0%	21.7%	27.1%

Customer Segment Gross Profit Report

Cardholder Results						
Customer Segment	**Best Cust.**	**Potential Best**	**New Cust.**	**Sub-Total**	**No ID**	**Total**
Sales	64,200	97,600	6,200	168,000	32,000	200,000
Gross Profit	17,000	24,479	1,545	43,024	11,200	54,224
Gross Profit %	26.5%	25.1%	24.9%	25.6%	35.0%	27.1%

TABLE 17: CUSTOMER PROFIT & LOSS REPORTS

The top report is a traditional departmental gross profit report showing results by department. The lower report, a customer segment gross profit report, shows us not the departments generating the sales, but the customer segments that do — the Best, Potential Best, and New Customers. Then, to balance the total of these customer segments with the company's total sales, another segment, NOIDs, is added. The NOID segment comprises all transactions with no cardholder identification. (NOID is the compression of "No ID".)

This approach allows the complete integration of customer and financial records, enabling us to move to a system of customer accounting that works in parallel and is intertwined with our financial accounting.

The primary benefit of this form of reporting is that it enables us to see the profitability of our different customer segments. This is particularly helpful when we allocate our marketing expenditures: we can now more readily see the returns, in sales and gross profits, for our efforts. (After all, we do market to customers, not products!)

Talking of profitability, you may have noticed the high gross profit percentage earned by the NOIDS in Table 17. This occurred because, in a two-tier price scenario, customers without cards (the NOIDs) do not receive the reduced prices and therefore generate higher profit margins.

Even though the customer segment report uses the abbreviated threshold segments (Best, Potential Best and New Customers) a few companies have gone even further and break out the results for all four of their DROP customer segments, providing them with a more detailed reading on the effectiveness of their marketing investments.

Customer segment reporting is common among businesses that capture all of their customer transactions (eg, warehouse clubs, catalog companies, and on-line retailers). But it's a new discipline for traditional retailers.

However, this method of reporting will become common-place among retailers when the majority of their advertising moves from mass to targeted communications—ie, when they truly become customer-centric businesses.

THE BOTTOM LINE

A simple way to classify customers is provided in the figure below:

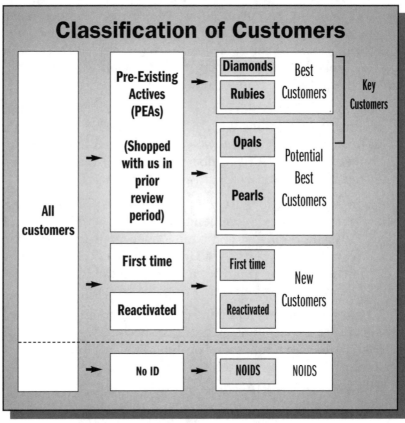

FIGURE 18: A CLASSIFICATION OF CUSTOMERS

PART II

THE DIVERSE PATHS OF LOYALTY

CHAPTER 4: THE POWER OF POINTS

The points path

Points are flexible and versatile. For some, they can be very expensive. However, a range of low-cost options is offered.

CHAPTER 5: A GIANT WITH A LASER FOCUS

The Tesco example

We learn how Tesco has built an information powerhouse on top of its simple points program.

CHAPTER 6: TWO-TIER PRICING

The price path

Two-tier price programs generate both information and incremental profits, making this a favored loyalty vehicle.

(continued)...

Chapter 7: Mission Marketing

The Big Y example

Big Y is a highly promotional, two-tier priced, loyalty card retailer. Its approach is so different from our other examples, reminding us there is no one best strategy.

Chapter 8: Best Customer Marketing

The Best Customer path

We learn why focusing on our Best Customers is the best strategy, whether our program features points or prices. Benefits are shown and suggestions are made on how a company can build its Best Customer numbers.

Chapter 9: Targeting the Primary Customer

The Boots example

We see how Boots has very carefully and creatively designed its loyalty program, available to all customers but of greatest interest and benefit to its Best Customers.

THE POWER OF POINTS

Chapter 4

The world is full of successful ideas that failed because they were not implemented well.

... Barbara Mowry

T he greatest potential strength of a points-based loyalty program is its flexibility. Its greatest potential weakness is its cost. Some companies take advantage of this flexibility; but many do not. Some companies construct their programs to minimize costs; but many do not. Let's begin this chapter with the most worrisome aspect: the cost.

COST

What do I mean by "a points program costing 1% of sales"? Today, particularly in Japan and Europe, programs are often structured along the following lines: one point is offered to cardholders for each $1.00 they spend; then, after 250 points have been accumulated, the cardholder receives a certificate for $2.50, which may be redeemed against a later purchase.

In Table 19, there are four different break-even calculations. The primary assumptions behind them are:

▼ 80% of the total sales are captured on the loyalty card (see row 1, all columns).

▼ Of the points that are issued, 80% are later redeemed (row 2, all columns).

▼ On the incremental sales gained as a result of the point program, the company earns 10%, 15%, 20%, and 25%, respectively (row 5, columns a-d).

Consider column a. If 80% of sales are captured on the loyalty card and customers redeem 80% of the points issued, then the points cost drops from 1.0% to 0.64% of total sales. (Calculation: 1.00% sales x 80% sales on card = 0.80% of total sales. This 0.80% of sales cost x redemption rate of 80% = 0.64% total sales, as seen in rows 14 and 15.) It also assumes the same 80/80 ratios apply to all incremental sales gained because of the program.

The third assumption—the profit on incremental sales—requires help from the accounting department. Thankfully, it's not a difficult estimation as it draws upon a company's past history. In column a, we are simply estimating that if the Profit Before Taxes (PBT) percentage on current sales is 3.0%, what will it be on any incremental sales?

As fixed costs are already covered in the 3.0% figure, one reasonable assumption is that on incremental sales, the PBT will be 10.0% of sales, a figure more than three times the existing profit rate. This translates into a profit (before taxes) of 10¢ on every incremental $1.00 of sales. Assuming these three factors (80%, 80%, and 10%), then to break-even:

▼ Sales have to increase from a base rate of $1,000 to $1,068.4, a 6.84% increase in sales (see column a, rows 6, 12, 28), and

▼ Profits (before the cost of the points) will need to rise to $36.84 (row 25), as the points cost on sales of $1,068.4, will be $6.84 (ie, row 26). The net of these two numbers ($36.84–$6.84) is $30.00 (row 27), the same profit earned as before launching the points program (row 13). In other words, to earn the same profit as before, given these three assumptions, an increase in sales of 6.84% is required!

Calculation steps are shown in rows 12-28.

	Assumptions		(a)	(b)	(c)	(d)
1	% Sales on card	%	80.0%	80.0%	80.0%	80.0%
2	% Points redeemed	%	80.0%	80.0%	80.0%	80.0%
3	Average cost of each	$	$0.01	$0.01	$0.01	$0.01
4	Profit Before Taxes (PBT)/Total Sales%	%	3.0%	3.0%	3.0%	3.0%
5	PBT % gain on each incremental sales %	%	10.0%	15.0%	20.0%	25.0%

	Results of above assumptions		(a)	(b)	(c)	(d)
6	Sales increase required to break even	%	6.84%	4.46%	3.31%	2.63%
7	Original PBT (before points)/Sales %	%	3.00%	3.00%	3.00%	3.00%
8	NewPBT (before points)/Sales %	%	3.45%	3.51%	3.54%	3.56%
9	New PBT (after points)/Sales %	%	2.81%	2.87%	2.90%	2.92%
10	Points cost/Sales %	%	0.64%	0.64%	0.64%	0.64%

11	**Calculations to get above results**	Calcn:		(a)	(b)	(c)	(d)
12	Assume base sales are		$	1,000	1,000	1,000	1,000
13	PBT before Points Program	4*12	$	30.00	30.00	30.00	30.00
14	Cost per point per $1 of Total Sales	1*2*3*	$	0.0064	0.0064	0.0064	0.0064
15	Point/Total Sales %	14/$1	%	0.64%	0.64%	0.64%	0.64%
16	**Detailed PBT Composition**						
17	PBT before Points Program	13	$	30.00	30.00	30.00	30.00
18	Points cost on base sales	12*15	$	(6.40)	(6.40)	(6.40)	(6.40)
19	PBT (after points cost) on base sales	17+18	$	23.60	23.60	23.60	23.60
20	Incremental sales needed to regain PBT	18/(5-15)	$	68.38	44.57	33.06	26.27
21	PBT % gain on each incremental sales $	5	%	10.0%	15.0%	20.0%	25.0%
22	PBT gain on incremental sales	20*21	$	6.84	6.69	6.61	6.57
23	Points cost on incremental sales	14*20	$	(0.44)	(0.29)	(0.21)	(0.17)
24	PBT (after points) on incremental sales	22+23	$	6.40	6.40	6.40	6.40
25	New Total PBT before points cost	17 +22	$	36.84	36.69	36.61	36.57
26	Total points cost	18 +23	$	(6.84)	(6.69)	(6.61)	(6.57)
27	New Total PBT after points cost	25+26	$	30.00	30.00	30.00	30.00
28	New Total Sales	12+20	$	1,068.4	1,044.6	1,033.1	1,026.3
29	**Sales increase required to break even**	6	%	**6.8%**	**4.5%**	**3.3%**	**2.6%**

TABLE 19: POINTS BREAK-EVEN CALCULATIONS

In other words, each point is worth one cent and is credited to the customer each time she spends $1.00. Such a points program is, in effect, a 1% rebate program, costing 1% of the retailer's sales.

What does that cost mean to the retailer? Table 19 shows a typical 1% points program in which 80% of the retailer's sales are captured on its loyalty card and, of the points issued on those sales, 80% are later redeemed by customers. *To break even with such a program, total company sales must increase by:*

➤ 6.8%, if incremental sales yield 10¢ profit per dollar

➤ 4.5%, if incremental sales yield 15¢ profit per dollar

➤ 3.3%, if incremental sales yield 20¢ profit per dollar

➤ 2.6%, if incremental sales yield 25¢ profit per dollar

This is a very powerful statement that every company with a points program needs to understand. (The steps involved and the appropriate validation calculations are set out on the two previous pages.)

The actual break-even point for any business will vary with its cost structure. Fortunately, it's a simple calculation and the three factors involved are easy to estimate (as shown in rows 1 to 5 of Table 19).

A company with a high profit/sales ratio typically finds it easier to achieve the breakeven point than one with a low profit/sales ratio because its incremental profit ratio is also usually higher. It's my observation that, today, many low margin retailers with a 1% points cost are not achieving a high profit rate on their incremental sales and are nowhere near achieving a 6.8% same-stores sales gain, year after year, from their programs. In other words, their points programs are losing money! In some cases, far too much.

How representative are the 80/80 assumptions?

The figures in Table 20 show the break-even sales increase required at various combinations of sales captured on the program, points redemption rates, and levels of profits earned on the incremental sales. They were derived using the methodology shown in Table 19. These ranges are typical of those that I see in retailers around the world. It shows that the breakeven requirements based on the 80/80 assumptions (row 5) are not significantly different from those of the other combinations on the other rows.

1	PBT % Gain on Each Incremental Sales $	10.0%	15.0%	20.0%	25.0%
2	**% Sales on Card/% Points Redeemed**				
3	70% - 80%	5.9%	3.9%	2.9%	2.3%
4	70% - 90%	6.7%	4.4%	3.3%	2.6%
5	80% - 80%	6.8%	4.5%	3.3%	2.6%
6	80% - 90%	7.8%	5.0%	3.7%	3.0%

Table 20: Summary of Break-Even Sales

Not all points programs are the same

Of course, not all retail and service sectors have a low- margin profit structure. Department stores, clothing chains, and restaurants, for example, typically enjoy higher margins than food retailers. Even within the same sector, profit margins range from high to low. For example, the major food retailers in the UK have a profit/sales ratio about three times higher than US food retailers. As indicated above, the higher the profit/sales ratio, the higher the incremental profit rate is likely to be and, therefore, the lower the sales gain required to breakeven.

This means that two competitors with different profit structures can offer identical point programs yet experience different impacts on their profits.

Note also that companies that enjoy high profit margins, such as restaurants, can place a different emphasis on their points programs. They can afford to be more generous. Thus, they often use points more often than low-margin retailers in direct sales-building activities.

It's fair to say, however, that regardless of the business sector we operate in, it's critical that we understand the underlying economics of our points program. A points program is a wonderful tool with which to elicit customer information. But it's important that it is structured in such a way that it has a low-cost impact on the business—and we can only know that if we understand its economics.

WHAT ARE THE ALTERNATIVES?

If a low margin retailer finds itself in the position outlined above—a 1% cost of points program with same-stores sales gains well below its break-even level—there are, fortunately, a number of alternative models to consider, which are set out below. Most of the companies described are capturing a high percentage of sales with their loyalty cards yet are successful in minimizing the cost of their points. They include:

The Ogino model: Ogino is a 30-store Japanese retailer with a highly successful points program. Ogino offers one point per ¥200 (US$2) on food and one point per ¥400 ($4) on non-food purchases, which gives a blended cost of less than half that of a typical 1% program. By significantly lowering the cost of its points program, Ogino has minimized the same-store sales gain needed to break even.

The Gerland's model: Gerland's, a 15-store food retailer in Houston, Texas, is a very creative practitioner of loyalty marketing. It has a two-tier price program on all items in its weekly circular and on selected items around the store.

(Two-tier pricing means that shoppers who choose not to present a loyalty card when shopping pay the regular shelf price; customers presenting a loyalty card pay the lower price.) In addition, Gerland's offers a points program that is an excellent example of flexibility. Points are offered not on the customer's transaction total, but on a varying number of high-margin items around the store. Whenever a cardholder has accumulated a total of 400 points, the checkout cashier automatically gives her a gift certificate entitling her to 5% off any subsequent transaction of her choice. The points on the high-margin products encourage customers to switch their purchases from lower-margin alternatives, thereby increasing the category's gross profit. The increased profit, in turn, pays for a large part of the points program.

The Clemens model: Clemens is a strong, progressive regional 19-unit chain based near Philadelphia, Pennsylvania. The company offers a two-tier price program similar to Gerland's, together with a points program that offers one point per dollar spent. The interesting twist is that each point has a redemption cost of only 0.2 cents, one fifth of the typical 1% program. Points are redeemable primarily on featured ad items. When the customer wishes to redeem points for a designated item in Clemens' biweekly circular listed at, say, $1.00, the cashier simply deducts 500 points from the customer's point balance. This, obviously, is a very low-cost points model. Its appeal is that it provides a benefit to customers for always presenting their card when shopping, thereby encouraging high usage.

The Yoshiya model: Yoshiya is a pioneering 11-store, Tokyo food retailer. Its points-based loyalty program has a unique feature. At the beginning of each month, Yoshiya advertises different point rewards for each day of the month. For example, on Tuesdays it may offer five points per ¥100 spent on seafood purchases while on Thursdays it may offer points based on a customer's total spending. Recently, the company added a new element: it began offering cardholders 600 two-tier priced items in addition to its points offers. What is attractive about this model is its flexibility. Yoshiya can change its program costs each month by changing the daily points offered and/or by moving the emphasis away from points towards its two-tier price program. The break-even point for its program changes each month in unison with changes in its program mix. In this way, Yoshiya has sidestepped the trap of being locked into a fixed cost points program.

The Busy Beaver model: This innovative 14-unit Pittsburgh, Pennsylvania-based do-it-yourself home improvement chain achieves a very high share of sales on its loyalty card with an elegantly simple program. It offers two-tier pricing on its dozen weekly specials. No other store prices are reduced. In addition, each card-based transaction has a sweepstakes entry automatically printed by the cash register attached to the bottom of the register tape, which shows the cardholder's name and card number. The customer simply drops the entry into a sweepstakes container near the front door when leaving. As an additional incentive to keep customers returning and to present their cards, Busy Beaver offers them rewards based on their purchases over a defined period. One recent offer earned a cardholder a gift certificate for $5.00 if her accumulated spending was $250 during a four-month period, escalating up to $400 if spending reached $10,000 (plus 5% on all spending over $10,000). This approach is akin to a points program but excludes rewards for low spending customers in the qualification period. The program also has more flexibility than the typical points program in that Busy Beaver can change both the rewards offer and length of the accumulation period as one period ends and before the next begins.

The two-tier pricing model: The last option is to replace the points program with a straight, two-tier pricing program. Dorothy Lane Market and Big Y, discussed elsewhere, are excellent examples of such programs. Two-tier pricing programs avoid the costs that usually come with a points program, but they don't enjoy the same degree of flexibility. That's why a number of retailers who use them add a low-cost points component, either on a short- or long-term basis, to their two-tier pricing program.

FILTERS

In addition to the approaches outlined above, another way to significantly lower the costs of a points program is by using filters.

Points given away that don't change customer behavior are both expensive and wasteful. Unfortunately, they form a considerable part of the cost of a straight 1%-of-sales points program. When a customer is offered one point for every dollar she spends, does this motivate her to significantly increase her spending? Not necessarily, as she is being given a gift of points from the company just for doing what she has always done, which illustrates the inherent waste in a flat 1%-of-sales program.

However, if she is offered points on her increased spending over, say, last year, it could well encourage her to spend more—which is really what the company was hoping to achieve when it set up the program. And the cost of points offered for incremental spending is usually not great if it results in a positive change in behavior.

Reducing the number of points given for unchanged or low value behavior is the most common way of applying filters to a program. These filters have two primary benefits. First, they minimize the cost of points that don't trigger higher spending thereby freeing up cash to be spent on more rewarding targets. Second, they help cut costs in areas where most customers won't feel the cut.

Examples of filters include:

Continente: An interesting filter appeared in the mid-1990s when one of Spain's leading retailers, the Continente hypermarket group, introduced its loyalty program. Designed by its talented marketing director, Iñaki Ereño, Continente had an underlying offer of five points per 500 pesetas spent in each transaction. To the customer, this appeared to be a 1% program, yet by applying some clever filters, Continente reduced its costs significantly.

In the first filter, spending that fell between the 500-peseta breaks earned no extra points. Thus, a transaction of 490 pesetas earned no points at all, and one of 510 or 990 pesetas earned the same five points. This filter reduced the cost of points from what appeared to be a 1% offer. It also encouraged some customers to spend more to break through the next reward threshold, thereby increasing sales.

A second seemingly minor, yet important, filter favored Continente's better customers. At each quarter's end, points that cardholders had earned were multiplied by factors of 0.8, 1.0 and 1.2, depending on the total number of points earned in the quarter. Low points totals were multiplied by 0.8; high points totals by 1.2. Only then were point totals converted into gift vouchers to be redeemed in its stores.

Base vs Bonus Points: Another filter, commonly used by European retailers, is to differentiate between Base Points (those earned on a customer's total spending) and Bonus Points (typically, those earned on promoted products when purchased). Thus, when retailers offers double points, say, for shopping on Wednesdays, only the Base Points are doubled; there is no doubling of any Bonus Points earned on products purchased around the store.

Automatic points expiration: Many companies trim their points costs by having expiration dates on outstanding points balances in inactive accounts. For example, at Yoshiya, both the customer's card and any outstanding points balance automatically expire if the card has had no activity in any consecutive 12-month period.

Seasonal points programs: Yet another very powerful filter that favors regular customers, minimizes costs, provides incentives to increase sales, and is very flexible is to have seasonal (ie, non-continuous) points programs. One major drawback of an on-going points program is that everyone, even the low-spending customers, will finally reach the required threshold spending level. Retailers can avoid this by having different points programs of defined duration during the year, offering specific rewards for different point totals redeemed.

BI-LO, a Mauldin, South Carolina-based food retailer, runs such limited-period points programs as a supplement to its highly aggressive two-tier price program. For several years, BI-LO has run a pre-Christmas points accumulation program (with customers' current points balance printed on their register tapes), offering one point per dollar spent. Points were redeemable for a range of appliances, popular as Christmas gifts or as something special for oneself. The 10 to 12 week accumulation period encouraged customers to consolidate their food buying at BI-LO to build their points balances, thereby increasing company sales. Of course, low spending customers didn't earn enough points for even the lowest threshold reward so no monies were spent on this segment. At the end of the period, all unused points expired.

Another loyalty pioneer successfully built each year's marketing program around three such limited-period points events: Easter (with an offer allowing customers to save points for an Easter ham, etc); the Hundred Days of Summer (Memorial Day to Labor Day) for points to be redeemed for summer products and gift certificates; and Thanksgiving (points accumulated for a free half or whole turkey). At the end of each promotional period, all unused points expired. Each program was a fresh start. One additional benefit with such a limited period promotion is that retailers have found that manufacturers are keen to participate by offering points on their products to help customers build their points totals.

VIPS Club: Another fascinating use of filters I recently discovered in Spain. The VIPS program covers the 11-fascia range of restaurants and shops owned by the Madrid-based

Sigla Group. The restaurants range from "five-fork" dining establishments to fast-food outlets. The group also includes stores selling general merchandise, ranging from books and music to gifts and photo processing. This high-growth company uses its program to drive group-wide sales.

The latest refinement of its VIPS Club (the rules are altered and new cards issued every two years) credits members with 3.3% of their purchases from any restaurant or store in the group. When members accumulate 15,000 pesetas (about US$80) they are sent a *VIPS Money Certificate* worth 500 pesetas (3.3% of 15,000). These can be redeemed at any of Sigla's diverse restaurants. However, because restaurants have low operating costs during non-peak times, they offer members double redemption value if they eat at such times.

Thus, Sigla's time-based filter is a win-win proposition: members who take advantage of these non-peak times receive added value, and Sigla sells additional meals at quiet times. This is in contrast to its previous two-year cardholder offer, a straight 5% program with no inducements for off-peak dining. From the group's bottom-line perspective, the new filtered program is more profitable while, at the same time, it provides its members with greater value.

FLEXIBILITY

Points appear "softer" than price reductions and are accepted more readily as inducements and rewards. We have found that customers perceive some offers as "bribes" or consider them crass if the inducement is in the form of a price-off coupon. Yet they accept them readily when offered as points, where the incentive element is less obvious. Aside from the cost of points, their flexibility and versatility in influencing behavior can be significant. Positioned properly, they can act as a tiebreaker when a customer is deciding where to shop on any given day. Some examples demonstrating the flexibility of points were given earlier, in the discussion on the cost of points. Here are more examples:

Goof Points: My favorite example of the flexibility of points as a reward vehicle is Superquinn's *Goof Points* program. To let customers know that the company was committed to significantly reducing the problems it was hearing about in its customer panels, Superquinn introduced a short-term program giving customers a 100-points certificate should they find any of fifteen common store-level problems (or *goofs*) when they shopped.

The nature of the program was such that they did not want customers feeling that they were spying on the employees, so none of the goofs involved finger pointing. Rather, the goofs were for general things such as finding a shopping cart with a wobbly wheel; discovering out-of-date products on the shelves or a burst sausage on display in the meat case; or finding that not all checkouts were open when there were checkout lines more than two customers deep.

Both the customers and the store management teams got behind the program with grace and humor, resulting in on-going operational improvements. In fact, the program was so successful that it has since become a permanent feature at Superquinn. But no longer does Superquinn reward customers just for finding the original fifteen problems; it now offers customers a 100-points certificate for *anything* they find wrong in their stores!

The goofs program has been transformed into an on-going, quality control program conducted weekly by over a quarter of a million quality control experts—the customers—who decide not only what will be inspected daily, but also what is acceptable quality. This is a truly remarkable way of receiving continuous, instant customer feedback—all carried out with an underlying sense of fun. It's a program that succeeds with points but would be unlikely to have similar success if the reward offered was a 60¢ cash voucher.

Reducing and increasing traffic: To ease customer congestion on Saturdays in one of its stores, one retailer encouraged customers to switch shopping days by offering double points on its quiet day, Wednesday. Double points have also been offered for shopping at quiet times of the day, such as 6–9 pm. Sanwa, a Tokyo food retailer, offers one point on every ¥200 (US$2) of purchases but gives double points on orders over ¥1,800 ($18) on Saturdays, as an inducement to build that day's business among its better customers. Such targeted incentives are much easier and cheaper to communicate and manage than widespread price changes in selected time periods. Operationally, points are easy to turn on and off.

Appearance rewards: Some companies offer selected customers points just for turning up at a store (where hopefully they will purchase something!). Such customers then have to keep returning to build their points balance to meet the earning threshold.

Christmas Club interest: Two global loyalty leaders offer points in lieu of interest on customers' Christmas Club monthly balances. These are programs where customers leave change from their transactions during the year and use it in December for their holiday shopping.

Signature items: Points are used as rewards for buying the company's signature items, avoiding an image-diluting price reduction on those items, yet having a comparable long-term sales-building effect.

Frequency: Points have been used effectively to build frequency. A major challenge for a business with small transaction sizes and low profit margins is to develop a loyalty program that is attractive to customers, and affordable.

Petrol retailers in particular face this challenge. In the Netherlands, Esso creatively uses the flexibility of points to solve the problem. On any transaction of at least 25 liters (about 6 gallons), Esso's cardholders receive points based upon the number of liters purchased. Double points (ie, a 100% points bonus) are given on a subsequent purchase if it is made within four days of the previous transaction; a 50% points bonus is given on a subsequent transaction if it is made within eight days; and a 10% points bonus is given on a subsequent transaction if made within twelve days. The calculations are easily and accurately made because members of Esso's Golden Tiger Card program are each issued a smart card containing a chip that records the date, details, and points earned in each transaction.

Petrol programs are similar to airlines' frequent flier programs: the employer pays for the purchase while the employee, who makes the purchase decision, collects the points. So, wherever possible, the employee is inclined to buy from the outlet offering the points.

The convenience store sector is another industry with small transaction sizes and low profit margins. Lawson, a 7,000-unit Japanese chain, has devised another imaginative solution, again taking advantage of the flexibility of points. Lawson offers cardholders one point per ¥1,000 (US$10) spent each month. Points—30, 50, 100, or 200—are redeemable for different levels of gifts, with the value of a point kept unclear to the customer.

However, for many cardholders the real appeal lies in Lawson's annual sweepstakes for cardholders in which 2,000 members win a week's vacation in Hawaii. But only those who have spent over ¥100,000 (about US$1,000) during the year are eligible. The company has designed a unique, low-cost way to encourage customers to want to present their card on their often low-value transactions. In return, Lawson has generated a rich database to which it can turn for deeper customer comprehension.

The Bic program: My last example to illustrate the flexibility of points is seen at another Japanese retailer, Bic Camera, a consumer electronics chain. Unlike food retailers, which have short periods between customer visits, electronic retailers can experience long gaps between visits. This greatly increases the chance of customer defection. (Out of sight, out of mind!)

To overcome this problem, Bic has built into its pricing and cost structure a "subsequent visit" points program. Each time a shopper uses her free Bic Points card, she is credited with points, redeemable on subsequent visits, which are based on the amount she spends and her method of payment. If she pays with cash, she receives a 10% credit in points (eg, for buying a camera for ¥10,000 she receives 1,000 points). If she buys the same item with a credit card the points credit is 8%, to allow for credit card costs. Each point is worth one yen. Accumulated points may be redeemed at any time.

Bic has thus created its own repeat-business reminder system—hurry back, as you always have a discount waiting for you! During the year, depending on the competitive situation and the company's sales needs, the 8% or 10% points reward offer is raised and lowered. In other words, a key element of Bic's loyalty program is its use as a simple, flexible promotional tool.

OTHER CONSIDERATIONS

As points are a marketing tool, we should always keep in mind that it's not what we, within our companies, think about our points program but it is what our customers think that's most important. It's easy to waste money otherwise. This was brought home to me when I was reviewing the survey findings of a large points-based client. The findings showed that:

- ❖ 95% of its customers were familiar with its card, and

- ❖ 90% of its customers had the loyalty card

However, despite these very favorable numbers:

❖ Only 20% of customers were aware of the additional one point per \$1 given on the company's extensive range of private label products;

❖ Only 30% were aware of the 1 point per \$1 given on total customer spending; and

❖ Some 80% were aware of the bonus points featured on items around the store.

The key finding in the survey was the huge awareness gap between two of the offers: points on total spending (30% awareness) and points on promoted products (80%). Fewer than one in three customers were even aware of a program that cost 0.7% of sales. Yet four out of five knew about a program that cost only 0.2% of sales. It was a vivid reminder to me of the value of offering points on products rather than on total spending.

The findings led to the immediate abandonment of the company's points on the private label program (which had only 20% awareness), saving a lot of money and having no negative sales effect.

Another lesson came from this experience: no matter how much we advertise and promote our loyalty program (or any other program) the message just doesn't get through to every customer. We can never over-communicate.

POINTS AREN'T "FUN MONEY"

It's so simple to design all sorts of creative and generous rewards using points. Points are easy to give away or "spend" by the marketing team (and by top management!) because they have a sense of "fun money" about them.

Therefore, to maintain an appropriate sense of reality, it's critical to quantify and incorporate the cost of issuance immediately into the financial system. The estimated value of a point must be calculated and all points issued must be billed each week as a cost to the business.

Further, as one purpose of a points program is to build company sales, points should be considered as an alternative to promotional pricing. In most companies, points and price reductions are complementary activities. Therefore, just as price markdowns are reflected in the company's weekly gross profit statement, so too should the costs of all points issued. It is inconsistent financial practice to treat price markdowns as a gross profit item yet treat points as an expense item (like, say, wages or utilities), which too many companies, unfortunately, still do. They should be treated as a cost-of-goods-sold item.

POINTS PROGRAMS SAVE APPLICATION COSTS

Points programs readily allow delayed registration, whereas two-tier price programs do not. There is no need for customers to ever have to line up to register for a points program. As seen at Tesco in the UK, customers wishing to join its points program can take an application form, with a loyalty card attached, from a display at the front of the store and can start earning points immediately. However, as Tesco cannot send these new cardholders their quarterly rewards certificates for points accumulated until customers have returned their completed application forms, there is an excellent incentive to mail in one's application.

The next step, which several companies are already planning, is to convert the application form, card, and benefits brochure into a shrink-wrapped package, charge a one-time fee for the card, and display it on a J-hook like a regular item of merchandise. The cashier activates the card at the time of purchase. Provided regular customers can see there is sufficient benefit in paying to join, they will happily do so. If customers were charged a reasonable fee for the package, but offered a refund if they spend, say, $500 within six months, this would discourage occasional shoppers from buying the package yet, at the same time, encourage regular shoppers, thereby minimizing program waste.

As one customer said during a research interview, a points program is simply "delayed gratification"—*buy now, get a reward later*—as when you have earned, say, 250 points. Assuming points are used in lieu of price reductions, another benefit accrues to the retailer: a permanent interest-free cash float, just like American Express enjoys with its issued, but unredeemed, Travelers Checks.

THE BOTTOM LINE

Points are the equivalent of real cash and must be treated, accounted for, and managed as such. Therefore, as much as possible, they should be used to encourage changes in customer behavior and not as rewards for existing behavior. Points have enormous flexibility. Our challenge is to creatively use that elasticity to assist us in achieving our business goals.

Every points proposal that involves spending company funds should be carefully analyzed in advance to assess its impact on the business. Points can be powerful—but they can also be expensive! It's critical that we understand the economics of our program.

We should also remember that, for most businesses, the primary purpose of a points program is to encourage customers to present their cards so that their activity can be recorded and understood. Just introducing a points program in the hope of profitably increasing sales—and not using the customer data—is like a dairy farmer who, after separating the cream from his milk, pours the cream down the drain. The richest part of the program is being wasted!

A GIANT WITH A LASER FOCUS

Chapter **5**

The best way to put distance between you and the crowd is to do an outstanding job with information. How you gather, manage, and use information will determine whether you win or lose.
... Bill Gates, *Business @ The Speed of Thought*

We do not believe in mass marketing anymore.
... Ian MacLaurin, Chairman, Tesco (1996)

Tesco is the largest food retailer in the United Kingdom, with annual group sales exceeding $US30 billion. This was not always the case. Back in early 1995, when Tesco was the first food retailer to launch a nationwide loyalty card program, the company was number two in sales behind card-skeptical Sainsbury's, who had held the sales title for decades. Within two short years, the situation had reversed. Tesco was firmly wearing the sales crown and Sainsbury's had introduced its own loyalty card.

From the beginning, Tesco's Clubcard was a success. It rapidly gained nationwide acceptance; of eight million magnetic-striped cards issued in the first year, five million were still in use early the following year. Five years later, one in three UK households had a Tesco card, with almost double the first year's number of active cardholders. Today, capturing over 85% of company sales, information from Tesco's

Clubcard is the pair of night vision goggles that help this pioneer see more clearly the realities of the competitive battlefield and the strategic options ahead.

A FLEXIBLE, EVOLUTIONARY APPROACH

Even though the Clubcard seemed to many customers to be a 1% points program, subtle qualifiers were included that significantly reduced the program's cost. Customers earned one point for every full £5 (approximately $7.50) in any transaction of £10 or more. This meant, for example, that a customer spending £8 received no points, while a customer spending £11 earned two points and those spending £19 earned three points. With almost half of Tesco's transactions being under £10 and having a big gap (£5) between earning thresholds, the company's points cost was significantly lower than a typical one point per £1 spent program. After its launch, to help offset the program's incremental costs, Tesco significantly cut back its traditional advertising budget.

Tesco sent each Clubcard member a quarterly points statement as long as she had 50 points or more (ie, she had spent at least £250). The statement included cash-back vouchers, one £2.50 voucher for each 50 points earned. Any unused points were carried forward to the next quarter.

Several years later, Tesco made the program simpler and easier to understand by switching from one point per £5 spent to one point per £1 spent, along with a corresponding change in the reward values. The new offer meant that a balance of 250 points now earned the cardholder a £2.50 voucher; a much simpler concept. Additionally, to help the customer build her points total more quickly, bonus points were offered on selected items around the store.

Tesco, being a high-margin food retailer (compared to US, not UK, retailers), did not have to significantly increase its sales to compensate for the additional costs involved in the program change. Even so, it did take the added step of increasing manufacturer participation in quarterly targeted offers to help offset the increase in its Clubcard costs.

This change meant that customers were now rewarded for showing their cards for all transactions, not just those over £10, which resulted in an increase in the share of sales captured on Clubcard. (In 1995, Tesco was capturing 70% of sales; five years later it was 85%.)

Using information from this deeper, richer customer database, the company stepped up its focus on building sales, customer retention, and improving the yield in many parts of the business: from advertising and pricing to real estate and new business development.

THE ROLE OF THE CLUBCARD

Terry Leahy, Tesco's CEO, states that the goal of the Clubcard is "to earn and grow the lifetime loyalty of the customer." It acts as a vehicle for Tesco to add value to customers in the form of services, product range, and prices as well as enabling the company to say "thank you" to its customers. In essence, its Clubcard is:

❖ A tool to understand the customer

❖ A way to communicate value

❖ A symbol of commitment

As with all global leaders in loyalty marketing, Tesco's understanding and use of its card has expanded as the value of its customer information has become more apparent.

During the first two years of Clubcard's existence, data usage was relatively simplistic: quarterly offers were made to customers in very broad categories. However, with two years of history in its database, Tesco began to take customer analysis seriously by developing sophisticated segmentation models. These models, based upon detailed analysis of actual customer behavior, became the foundation for subsequent marketing developments. The time for raising the curtain on the Second Act, with its heavy reliance on the understanding and use of customer data, was at hand.

THE *SECOND ACT:* INFORMATION-BASED RETAILING

Certain events stand out as we follow Tesco's evolution from a food retailer into an information-based media company, a term used by Clive Humby, the chairman of Dunnhumby, to describe Tesco today.

1995   Launch of Clubcard

1996   Launch of Clubcard Plus

1997   Launch of Banking / Financial Services

1999   National rollout of Home Delivery

2000   Strengthening of Tesco's web offering

2001   Buys majority stake in Dunnhumby

Sixteen months after the launch of Clubcard, Tesco introduced Clubcard Plus, an alternative card carrying a payment feature. It was, in effect, a debit card with the best interest rates available in the UK. The success of this venture encouraged management to move into banking and financial services the following year.

How do financial services relate to a food retailer? Through convenience, information, and cost. Consumers visit supermarkets several times a week. Depositing and withdrawing cash while in the store is a convenience as it eliminates the need for a separate trip to a bank.

With information derived from its loyalty card and enriched by appended external demographic data, a food retailer can readily develop profiles of customers who would most likely be interested in basic banking services as well as an array of related options, ranging from car loans and pension savings programs to insurance for all types of needs — car, home, travel, and even pets.

Without a doubt, having customer information gives a company a competitive edge. It costs Tesco significantly less than half of what it costs a bank to acquire a financial services customer. Additionally, Tesco's negotiating power for favorable insurance rates for its 10 million active cardholders is extremely strong.

Thus, *agentry*—thinking and acting as the customer's agent—has blossomed as the way of operating at Tesco. In its food buying, Tesco had, for many years, been using its buying muscle to get low prices for its customers. Now that it had actual information about its customers, Tesco could act on their behalf in any related area. As Tim Mason, Tesco's marketing director told me, "We move into new markets where we believe we can create value for customers consistent with our values."

Banking and insurance were its first foray. Since then, Tesco has aggressively worked on building up its website to provide not only home delivery of food, but also a diverse offering including books, music, computers, TVs, VCRs, and videos. Clothing and home furnishings are expected to follow. Even using its agentry power to offer new cars at the lowest market prices seems within reach and various tests have already been made in this area.

So here we see a major retailer evolving in its strategic thinking and direction from being an outstanding food retailer to being an information-driven business, constantly searching for ways to act as the value-adding agent for its customers, wherever that may lead it.

Thinking as the customer's agent reflects itself in many ways. One example is seen in its home shopping service, now available throughout all but the more remote parts of the United Kingdom. Tesco uses its Clubcard to link a customer's on- and off-line behavior. Tesco already knows an existing customer's purchase behavior, so when she logs on to place a home delivery order for the first time, she isn't overwhelmed by 20,000 products listed in alphabetical order. Instead, her shopping list begins with her "favorites", items drawn from her recent shopping history in the store. That is truly using technology to make the customer's shopping experience more pleasant.

' Further, the customer's shopping history, both off-line and on-line, is used to create suggestions that appear while the customer is placing her order. With customer-centric thinking such as this, it should be no surprise to learn that Tesco has become the world's largest home delivery service.

HARNESSING THE DATA

Imagine an active database containing shopping data from one in every three households throughout the whole country. Data not just related to food spending in stores and on home delivery, but also financial services and a diverse range of non-food offerings. As Bill Gates suggests, what potential lies therein for putting distance between you and the crowd!

To ensure that this rich lode is thoroughly mined, some years ago Tesco outsourced the task to London-based data analysts, Dunnhumby, with the challenge of both optimizing the information and working closely with the operating side of the business to profitably apply their findings. Dunnhumby's 24-person analytical team did just that. So well, in fact, that Tesco recently bought a majority shareholding in this independent data-analysis company.

A careful analysis of customer data helps Tesco in so many ways. Let's start with its home delivery service. Tesco has learned, for example, which of these customers are new to Tesco (ie, incremental business); to what degree customers using home delivery change their store-based and total spending; and, by comparing customers' on- and off-line purchases, what the purchase resistance areas are in home delivery that need to be overcome.

Another very creative use of customer insight was applied several years ago. One of Tesco's key objectives is to be a price leader in the market place. How could this be accomplished at minimal cost?

It started by identifying those customers who had a large share of reduced-price items in their baskets and were, therefore, defined as the most price-sensitive. A study of this group's purchase behavior found that about 70 items comprised 40% of their purchases; these were the price sensitive shoppers' key items. So, rather than reducing prices across-the-board on 500 to 1,000 items—the traditional retailer's approach to pursuing a low-price perception—Tesco lowered prices significantly only on this smaller group of items that were important to their most price-sensitive shoppers. Result: a better price perception at the least cost.

Actual behavior is also used as a backdrop to the customer feedback sessions held every day in different parts of the company. Marrying attitude and behavior is the ideal way to close the loop on customer comprehension.

I have heard Tesco's Clubcard described as "a reward scheme that provides the data and a platform for promotion, while it is customer segmentation that provides the language and imagination to drive the program forward." With Dunnhumby's help, Tesco has taken segmentation to an art form and has the communications flexibility to deliver appropriate offers to the many different customer subsets in its database. This sophistication is seen in its quarterly voucher mailings.

Each year, Tesco mails over 36 million reward statements with up to 150,000 variations each quarter. The variations are both apparent and subtle, ranging from the product offer (ie, which customers receive which offers at what price) to the content of the letter and to the way it is personalized.

Along the bottom of these quarterly mailings are the cash-back vouchers. For example, there may be a £2.50 and a £1.50 voucher because the cardholder had a balance of over 400 points at the end the quarter. On the right hand side of the mailer are six product offers. These vary by customer, based upon what she has bought in the past.

A regular customer typically receives five *reward offers* and one *incentive offer.* An occasional customer typically receives two reward and four incentive coupons. Reward certificates offer items that a customer has bought in the past at very aggressive prices. An incentive certificate is for an item Tesco thinks the customer might like to try, based upon her purchasing history. The redemption rate of the cash vouchers exceeds 90%, while that for products grows each year as Tesco keeps refining its segmentation techniques.

SEGMENTATION

Effective targeting of individualized offers requires a quick matching of customers and offers. Tesco has done this by segmenting its customer base into sets of profiles. For example, a customer may fit into the following profile:

- ❖ Medium to high share of requirements
- ❖ Spends £70 to £80 per week
- ❖ Regular weekly shopper
- ❖ Weekend shopper
- ❖ Fresh and ready meals
- ❖ Promotionally aware
- ❖ High brand loyalty

Customers with each of these characteristics have broadly similar shopping and spending behavior and are, accordingly, targeted with similar offers.

Various approaches have been used to develop Tesco's primary, secondary, and tertiary segments. One primary approach breaks customers down according to their lifestyle, with monikers suggesting the type of household in the cluster. You can readily conjure up who may populate the following clusters:

- Making Pennies Work (ie, price sensitive)
- Better-Off Family Meals
- Conservative Quality
- Staple Family Meals
- Convenience Cooks
- Traditional Living
- Good Cuisines
- Quick Meals

The second approach has customers segmented based upon which of six primary lifestages they are currently in:

- Young Adults
- Old Adults
- New Families
- Old Families
- Pensioners
- Students

Lifestage segmentation has been particularly helpful to Tesco. For example, it has aided the company identify the most appropriate customer targets for financial services and subclub offers (eg, baby club, pet club). It has also assisted in refining the product range offered (eg, which stores should receive the finest premium products or the widest assortment of organics) and in selecting appropriate in-store facilities (eg, extra seating) throughout the chain. This segmentation approach is also the foundation underlying the many editorial variations of the Clubcard magazine, which is mailed regularly to cardholders.

The third primary segmentation approach is loyalty-based. Customers are classified based upon various combinations of how recently they last shopped, how frequently they have shopped, and how much they have spent over time at Tesco.

These three primary approaches are then integrated to develop a range of combinations and permutations to better describe the many different faces of Tesco's customer universe. Then add other filters to this extremely sophisticated level of segmentation, like the television viewing region in which the customer lives, and you begin to get an idea of how laser sharp this retail giant's targeted customer mailings really are.

THE BOTTOM LINE

Tesco is a company that understands that information is more powerful—and more profitable—than ignorance. Its appreciation and intelligent use of its rich customer database has clearly positioned the company as one of today's grand masters of data analysis.

Recognizing the value of information, Tesco recently offered access to its database (excluding customer details) to its suppliers. For a fee, a manufacturer can now analyze where its products sell best, against which competitors, and to which types of customers. For example, in conjunction with Tesco, a manufacturer can test different shelf presentation ideas and pricing tactics and measure the impact on sales and profits. Such lessons will, in due course, bring even further benefits to Tesco.

The broadening of its business vision has been enabled by the knowledge and insights bubbling from its cauldron of customer data—whose primary source is a simple, plastic loyalty card.

Given that Tesco is now truly an information-driven retailer, it will be interesting to see how it evolves from here and what surprises it will present us with next—in its Third Act.

A RETAILER'S VIEW

How does one of the world's largest retailers view its loyalty card program? I asked Tim Mason, marketing director of Tesco, how he would answer the two questions asked of the other global leaders.

Tim, what's your bottom line on the Tesco Clubcard?

"Our goal is to create value for customers to earn their lifetime loyalty. You can only do this customer by customer by being relevant and attractive to them personally. It's very difficult to do and literally impossible if you don't have a loyalty card."

Why, then, don't all retailers have a loyalty card program?

"I suppose the short answer is because not all companies share our goal. I'd like to meet one which did but didn't know the names of its customers."

Chapter **6**

The art of taxation is to pluck the goose with the least amount of hissing.
    ... Jean Baptiste Colbert (Louis XIV's Finance Minister)

If everything you try works, you are not trying hard enough.
    ... Gordon Moore, co-founder of Intel

While points-based loyalty card programs have the advantage of greater flexibility, price-based programs have the advantage of lower costs. As a general rule, a well-constructed price-based program not only increases the gross profit percentage more than a points-based program, it also captures a higher share of sales.

When we talk about price-based programs, we are referring to its most common manifestation: two-tier pricing. Two-tier pricing is simple, both in theory and practice: a wide range of advertised and unadvertised items are sold at a reduced price to customers who presents their loyalty card. Regular shelf prices are charged in transactions without a card. Typically, the card is free and available to anyone who has completed the application form.

Two-tier pricing originated in the United States where food retailers have very low profit margins (1-2% of sales). When loyalty card programs appeared on the scene in the 1980s, the idea of adding a new, permanent cost in the form of points was unsettling—particularly then, as the industry had recently extracted itself from a long era of high-cost trading stamps. Another attraction of two-tier pricing for food retailers at that time was the hope that suppliers would pay for many of the cardholder price markdowns.

In contrast, programs based on points originated in Europe where food retailers have higher profit margins and where retailers felt that points were more compatible with that continent's more egalitarian culture. Today, now that the strengths and weaknesses of both approaches are better understood, we see both price- and points-based programs, and various combinations of the two, used in all parts of the world. We have learned that there is no one best strategy; what is best depends upon a company's unique culture and its competitive situation. However, there is one guideline every company should follow: whatever vehicle you choose, build into it as much flexibility as possible for you will, without question, want to change it at some stage.

THE EVOLUTION OF TWO-TIER PRICING

Back in the late 1980s, when loyalty marketing was just beginning among US food retailers, the pioneers started with two-tier pricing on several hundred items. Over the years, as confidence increased, this number grew. Today, more committed retailers signal to customers from day one that, with a wide range of two-tier priced items, their new loyalty card program is a vital part of the company's offer.

For example, several years ago, Pleasanton, California-based Safeway launched its loyalty card in its Denver, Colorado, division with a big bang. Its program featured, beginning with the launch date:

❖ Every item in its weekly advertisement required a Safeway Club Card to get the lower price.

❖ All price markdowns (Temporary Price Reductions, Manager's Specials, etc) in its stores required a Club Card to get the lower price.

Combined, the above comprised over 3,500 items—more than 10% of the store's offering required a Safeway Club Card from the first day of the card's existence—a clear message to customers of the company's commitment!

At the same time, to encourage customers to spend more of their food budget with Safeway, the company offered a 5% off gift certificate for every $250 that customers spent during the first three months of the new program. These certificates were issued to customers on-line, real-time, through Safeway's point-of-sale system. A heavy barrage of radio and television commercials, supported by colorful "rolling billboards" (Safeway's description of its repainted tractors and trailers), rounded out the communication side of the new program.

Within two weeks of launch, 80% of sales were being captured on the card, highlighting the second of the two major benefits of a two-tier price program: high card usage.

We have found that a customer is more inclined to present her loyalty card when there is an immediate cash discount available than if she is offered a small quantity of points redeemable at some later date. Therefore, the greater the number of items around the store with two-tier price tags, the greater the potential cardholder savings and, therefore, the greater the likelihood of card usage by customers.

WHERE SOME OF THE LOYALTY CARD PROFIT GAINS COME FROM

Such a high percentage of a store's product range with two-tier prices seems expensive to those unfamiliar with loyalty card programs. It isn't. Actually, offering all advertised specials and Temporary Price Reductions (ie, temporary one-to-three month price reductions offered to retailers by suppliers) on a two-tier price basis increases gross profits. For example, if you are capturing 80% of your sales via your card, then 20% of your sales are sold at full price. This includes the two-tier items that, prior to the card program's introduction, would have been sold at the lower price to everyone—but not any more.

Among the food retailers I have studied, this has meant an increase in their gross profit percentage of about a half percent (0.5%) of sales if "only" 80% sales trigger price reductions. This gain is significant in the light of food retailers' low profit margins. In the US, for example, where many food retailers have a profit-before-taxes-to-sales ratio of 2.0%, an increase in the gross margin percentage of 0.5% is the equivalent of a 25% profit increase, all other things being equal.

But all other things aren't equal. When a loyalty card program is being planned, that's the time to clean out tired, old programs. These are either phased out prior to the new program launch and/or eliminated amidst the noise of the new program's launch. The types of programs jettisoned include double or triple coupons; 30-50% off greeting cards; entitlement programs such as senior citizen programs; 10% off all pre-priced items in the store; double your money back meat and produce guarantees; and automatic competitive ad-matching.

For some companies, the reduction or elimination of such programs provides a significant amount of funds that can be redirected to tactical card-related promotions. It's important to note, however, that the removal of such programs is not necessarily permanent. Most can later be offered as promotions from time to time or on certain days or weeks. The critical difference is that it provides you with a pool of profit margin which you can use flexibly—when, where and as you need it—and not as an under-appreciated customer entitlement. And, of course, any unused portion flows to your bottom line. Initially, many companies use the savings from the removal of these programs to help fund their program's launch.

Another important one-time source of profit gain comes in the transition period as companies move towards the goal of 80% of sales being captured on the card. If the transition is slow—several months rather than several weeks—a significant share of sales are at full margin.

Other potential gains occur when slow-moving, high-profit margin items around the store are included in the two-tier program. When the prices on these high-margin, slow sellers are reduced, their unit sales increase, often at the expense of the lower-margin (faster-moving) items, thereby increasing the company's overall gross profit!

A pure points program doesn't achieve these benefits. In fact, programs that issue points based on total sales add a permanent layer of cost to the business, which has to be paid for by an increase in sales, as explained earlier in Chapter 4.

Two-tier pricing is, therefore, a very cost-effective way of capturing a high share of customer data, the primary underlying purpose of a loyalty card program. It is easy to understand how a food retailer with a well-planned and well-executed loyalty card program increases its sales and profits in the program's launch year. It should also be no surprise that the majority of testimonials of strong profit gains reported in the Introduction to this book were from retailers with two-tier price programs.

THE DOWNSIDE OF TWO-TIER PRICING

As with every marketing program, two-tier pricing has a downside. The primary problem occurs at the checkouts, when a customer says she wants the lower cardholder prices but does not have her card. To minimize this occurrence, four main approaches are used:

❖ Offer cards that can be added to a customer's key ring, as few people shop without their keys.

❖ Install a card number look-up facility in each store so that a forgetful customer can have her card number keyed into her transaction, triggering the discounts earned on that order. Unfortunately, this is not a speedy process and can hold up checkout lines.

❖ When a customer forgets her card, have the cashier sign the customer's register tape, circle the order's potential discount (shown in small print on the bottom of the tape), and invite the customer to present the tape on her next visit with her card and the discount will be refunded at that time.

❖ Enforce a strict policy of *no card, no discount.*

Another concern with two-tier pricing occurs in tourist areas. Where a two-tier price retailer has stores with high tourist traffic the card program can be a costly irritant when an out-of-town shopper, unaware of the card program rules, expects the lower prices when checking out but learns she isn't eligible for them unless she signs up for a card. The whole front-end process, in the height of the busy tourist season, is slowed as the newcomer completes an application form for a card she may use only once or on just several more occasions. This situation means high card processing and data storage costs for customers unlikely to be regulars.

Unless the retailer really wants the names and addresses of these tourists, one common solution is to offer during the holiday season a continuity program, such as a 5%-off certificate for every $250 of total spending, and to temporarily halt two-tier pricing, ie, make the reduced prices available to every shopper.

This approach will still provide transaction information on the majority of sales as it continues to reward regular customers for presenting their cards. It is also attractive enough to encourage longer-staying, higher-spending tourists to apply for a card so that they, too, can earn rewards based on their total spending during their stay—and the retailer can learn more about these special customers.

Some companies ask their cashiers in tourist areas to swipe a "house card" for customers that don't have a card when checking out. This is not recommended as the data is of little value and the practice is hard to discontinue after the tourist season ends, leading to a significant amount of what are called "phantom sales" in the company's database.

Another isolated, but real, concern occurs when a store is in a neighborhood with a high number of people who, for diverse reasons, are reluctant to provide details about themselves, even their names and addresses. Yet they want the lower prices and the retailer wants their business. Some of these people are apprehensive even about using an unidentified card. Where the number of such people is significant, a two-tier price program may not be appropriate.

One possible alternative in this situation is a series of year-round, Busy Beaver-type continuity programs based on total customer spending *(see page 72)*. Those who are prepared to present a card with their transactions receive rewards based on their total spending so the company gains an insight into a section of its customer base. Those who are apprehensive about using a card miss out on these total spending rewards but are able to buy all items at their promoted prices because there is no two-tier card pricing.

These issues seem more common among price-based loyalty card programs than points programs because when a customer misses out on price reductions she often feels she is losing something immediate and tangible, something that is her "right". Points, by contrast, are often seen as an intangible, low-value add-on. When a customer doesn't earn them, there is not the same emotional response.

WHAT KEEPS CUSTOMERS INTERESTED?

"What do you do to keep customers interested in a two-tier price program?" is a question I am often asked. Two concerns usually prompt the question. First, is two-tier pricing enough to encourage each customer to happily present her card at each transaction or at least to do so with no feeling of irritation? Second, does it encourage a customer to keep returning to your stores?

In answering, we have to keep in mind that the primary purpose of a loyalty card is to gather customer information so that we can make better business decisions. These decisions range from providing a better customer experience to reallocating our marketing investments to achieve better economic returns. Reallocation means that some customers will receive more favorable offers than others. This goes to the heart of the first concern, as stated above. We seek to capture information on a very high proportion of our sales — but then, as we saw at Dorothy Lane, we turn around and focus our efforts on the top 30% of our customers who give us 75% of our sales — because that's where we achieve the best yield on our marketing investment. In all world-class loyalty programs, the top 30% do enjoy benefits over and above the basic two-tier price program. It's the bottom 70% who often don't see many of these additional benefits simply because, in most cases, offering special benefits to this group is poor economics for the retailer.

So the real challenge is how to encourage the lowest spending 70% of our customers, who generate 25% of our sales, to happily keep presenting their cards. To them, the typical two-tier price program is not very different from the days before the program was introduced, when they didn't have to present a card at all to get the same low prices.

The issue is to show these customers, at minimal cost to the company, that there is value in *always* presenting their cards. In the next chapter, you will see how Big Y successfully accomplishes this goal. It uses a number of tactics, including making the card appealing to both its high- and low-spending customers with crazy promotions, such as its *Buy 1 Get 2 Free* crowd-pleasers. It also has a biennial Education Express program that appeals to a wide range of customers, from young families to grandparents, covering all spending levels. Further, it has a discount program arrangement with a broad range of entertainment and education facilities throughout three New England states, whereby Big Y customers are charged a lower entrance fee, simply by presenting their *Express Savings Club* cards. Underpinning all of this, through its regular weekly ads, Big Y communicates and reinforces the value of its card to every customer.

THE BAKER'S APPROACH

Baker's, a regional chain based in Omaha, Nebraska, built strong interest in its Value Card among all cardholders through a variety of strong community events. Stephen Zubrod, the force behind these marketing and branding efforts, described to me some of these highly popular activities. He explains how, one year, Baker's arranged *Two Buck Tuesdays* with the local baseball team, the Omaha Royals.

On any Tuesday night when there was a home game, anyone with a Baker's card could buy four tickets for $2 (one purchase per family) as opposed to the regular $8 single ticket price. This extra-special low price was triggered at the box office upon presenting a Value Card. Nearby, a special scanner allowed cardholders to swipe their cards, registering to enter that night's sweepstakes. Prizes were typically trips to Kansas City to see a major league team, the Kansas City Royals, play.

Then, during a lull in the fourth inning, officials would go to the center of the field and ask all spectators with a Value Card to stand up and take out their cards (a very impressive sight!) as they announced the winner from all the cards that were scanned that night.

What a great way to add value to your card and, at the same time, encourage non-customers to start shopping at your company! Zubrod told me that in his entire marketing career he had never witnessed such a voluntary buy-in into a retailer's brand. The promotion was also great for the Royals, giving them greater hometown exposure and filling the stadium on the slowest night of the week. It also increased concession sales, which helped compensate for the discounted tickets.

Baker's developed a similar win-win relationship with the Nebraska Furniture Mart, a huge and highly successful Omaha store. All Baker's Value Card holders were invited to visit the Mart on any Tuesday evening in February for a private Value Card sale with significant discounts. In addition, attending Value Card members were entered into a sweepstakes for a free kitchen. Again, this partnership provided a special benefit to all Value Card holders.

Quite a different promotion was Baker's BOGO promotion with the local Henry Doorly Zoo. As the zoo is the second most popular tourist attraction in Nebraska, its management didn't want to introduce discounting at the zoo's entrance ticket boxes, yet it was keen to broaden its attendance pool. With the help of a local food manufacturer, ConAgra's Healthy Choice, and the full support of CEO Jack Baker, a much-needed giraffe was purchased for the zoo. It was given the name BOGO. Then, throughout the summer, any cardholder could buy zoo tickets at any of Baker's 15 stores on a Buy-One-Get-One (BOGO) Free basis, good for any Thursday admission.

At the same time, Healthy Choice supported this promotion—to meet BOGO the new giraffe—with a series of Buy-One-Get-One (BOGO) Free displays of its products in Baker's stores. By enthusiastically getting behind this promotion, Healthy Choice's volume soared, as did that of other manufacturers who also participated in Baker's summer BOGO promotion.

Everyone was a winner: the zoo, the supporting manufacturers, Baker's, and most importantly, Baker's customers. In this and the other two promotions featuring its card, Baker's promoted the partnership in both its circulars and stores as events open to all cardholders. *The message: this truly is a Value Card for everyone.*

OTHER APPROACHES

Other successful approaches used to remind customers of the value of always presenting their card include:

❖ Regular in-store sweepstakes with one entry per transaction

❖ Tiered spending programs (spend $250 in 10 weeks and receive a 5%-off certificate or spend $500 and receive a 7½%-off certificate, etc)

❖ Continuity pricing programs (eg, after every 12 items of this product that you buy during the next 6 months, we'll send you a $5 gift certificate)

❖ Subclubs (eg, a Baby Club or Pets Club)

❖ Simply reminding customers why they should always present their cards (as we saw in Figure 2, page 22)

❖ A regular reinvigoration of your program with fresh signage and advertising along with an employee re-commitment program

The answer to the second concern, "Does it encourage a customer to keep returning to your stores?" is "Possibly". It does only if the prices for cardholders are competitive.

We must always remember that the two-tier pricing proposition is simply the underlying program. Using the information generated, we develop programs aimed at building retention, frequency, and spending among our better customers, the primary beneficiaries of a two-tier pricing program.

We will return to this subject in Chapter 8, when we talk about our Best Customers.

MISSION MARKETING

Chapter 7

As long as we can differentiate ourselves from our competitors and adapt to a changing environment, we will never lose customers.
... Toshifumi Suzuki, CEO, Ito-Yokado (1995)

Every successful large business in existence was once a small business based on an idea of what the future should be.
... Peter Drucker

Imagine a loyalty program whose introduction was prompted not by customer loyalty but by operational issues.

Imagine a company that understands the power of simplicity, consistency, and focus, and then moves quickly to have all marketing activities revolve around its loyalty card to maintain this concentration.

Imagine a company that defines its vision of loyalty marketing as: *Mission Marketing—an all out frontal assault on the competition with our best weapon, the Express Savings Club. Every marketing program we develop has one mission—to promote our Club. It is a religion for us, not just another promotion.*

Imagine a company where, six times a year, all senior officers, including the CEO, COO, the Senior Vice Presidents of Operations and of Merchandising, and Vice President of IT, meet to discuss just one agenda item: How can we make our *Express Savings Card* program better?

Big Y Foods, based in Springfield, Massachusetts, is that company. At Big Y, all marketing decisions are evaluated based on whether or not they support its *Express Savings Club*. Every new program must improve and advance its loyalty card. As the folks at Big Y say: "Mission Marketing is not for the meek or faint of heart."

BIRTH OF THE EXPRESS SAVINGS CLUB

In 1990, the company was faced with the challenges of a very competitive, highly promotional marketplace. State law mandated that every grocery item sold at a special price had to be physically price marked, which added a heavy labor burden to this highly promotional chain.

On top of that, the northeastern section of the United States was mired in a long-running coupon frenzy. Not only did manufacturers offer a vast array of coupons to customers but so, too, did the leading food retailers. Handling all of those additional pieces of paper added significantly to front-end labor costs while customers complained about clipping all of these coupons.

After playing with many ideas, Big Y hit upon the idea of a loyalty card as a way to extricate itself from this costly situation, to clearly differentiate its stores, and to provide a clear marketing course for the future.

Big Y's creation, the *Express Savings Club* card, was elegantly simple in design. Launched in 1991, the supporting publicity heavily stressed its four cornerstones:

- ❖ No more coupons to clip
- ❖ Up to five of any advertised Club item can be purchased (in any one transaction)
- ❖ No minimum purchase was required (minimum purchases were common practice at that time)
- ❖ Free membership (a "dig" at the newly emerging membership-based warehouse clubs)

Since then, Big Y has stuck with these four simple tenets with great success. Store numbers more than doubled in the following decade and sales more than tripled. Big Y's World Class Stores, which average 60,000 square feet in size, are among the finest food stores in the United States. In the center of its stores are food courts, full of wonderful smells and taste treats. Big Y offers an outstanding array of bakery items. Its fruit and vegetables are consistently attractive and fresh. Its fish purchasing arrangements ensure consistently fresh fish. Only top-grade beef is sold. Like Dorothy Lane and Superquinn, Big Y Foods is not just an ordinary supermarket chain—it's a food store offering world-class fresh foods.

THE CRAZY EDDIE OF FOOD RETAILING

This billion-dollar retailer has succeeded by being true to its beliefs. Unlike Dorothy Lane and Superquinn, Big Y has always been a highly promotional company. Every week, local residents read its large and colorful 8-10 page advertisements, which have headline grabbers such as:

10¢ Sale!

25¢ Sale!

Breakfast Savings!

Super Express Deals!

Frozen Food Savings!

Lowest-Price-Ever Sale!

Unlimited Triple-Coupon Sale!

With Our Express Card Earn Double Points For Your School!

Buy One, Get One Free!

Buy Two, Get Three Free!

Buy One, Get Two Free!

When I was a student in the 1970s, there was a New York electronics retailer, Crazy Eddie, who had a mammoth reputation for outrageous prices. To me, Big Y is the Crazy

Eddie of food retailing. Fortified with the knowledge gained from its *Express Savings Club* card, Big Y has cracked the code on how to successfully run *Buy One, Get Two Free* promotions. In fact, the company has eight such promotions each year. Big Y is the only retailer in the world to successfully do this.

Imagine your local supermarket offering a *Buy One, Get Two Free* sale of such items as fresh whole chickens, large white eggs, Coca-Cola, Pepsi, Ginger Ale, bath tissue, bottled water, canned tuna, salad dressing, and paper towels. These items are typical of the items that Big Y offers (buy up to five, get up to ten free), and act as powerful magnets to existing and new customers alike.

On the surface, Big Y's approach appears to be mass marketing at its best: large, eye-popping advertisements with specials available to all who present their *Express Savings Club* card. And it is. However, Big Y also runs a parallel, *sotto voce,* Best Customer reward program in its stores.

TOKENS AND POGS

In differentiated marketing (offering different rewards to different customers), the biggest obstacle is perfecting a low-cost communication vehicle. Big Y has broken this cost barrier with a "coin", or token, program. Rather than using the relatively high-cost postal service, the company uses a deceptively simple system of colored, coin-sized tokens.

When an *Express Savings Club* card is swiped at any checkout, a message may appear on the cashier's screen prompting her to present the customer with a specific colored token. The front of the token reads: "Big Y Express Reward ... Thanks For Your Loyalty." On the reverse, it states: "Big Y's *Express Reward* ... Present To Cashier."

Big Y has never publicly explained how customers qualify for rewards under this program. ICL, Big Y's point-of-sale system provider, however, did provide clarification in a recent news release:

Another unique Big Y promotion is "Coins." Depending on purchases, shoppers get special coins—there are four different colors—that the shopper can redeem for a selection of free or discounted items. There are several different items offered per color of coin every promotion period, and the different coins then act as a sort of "wild-card coupon".

The release states that tokens are given to customers based upon their spending at Big Y. In other words, it's a Best Customer program. The tokens (the different colors have a hierarchy of values) are redeemable for specially identified items around the store and often include Big Y's signature items, such as its French bread, chocolate cake, freshly-made pizza, and its specially-flavored rotisserie chicken. As the tokens have no expiration date, customers can choose when they wish to redeem them.

With no announced rules as to how much a customer must spend to earn the different colored tokens, the marketing department obviously enjoys enormous tactical flexibility in their distribution. I have no doubt Big Y uses its store-issued token system to do everything that other companies do with their significantly more expensive mail-based communications, such as targeting "at risk" customers with special rewards when a new competitor enters the market.

Like any outstanding retailer, Big Y leverages its points of difference, its tokens being one of them. For example, just before Thanksgiving, Big Y identifies its Best Customers and triggers its cashiers to give one of two colored tokens. One token is for a free turkey; the other for a ten-dollar discount on a Thanksgiving turkey of the customer's choice. Like Dorothy Lane, Big Y believes in giving free or heavily discounted turkeys as a reward to those who demonstrated loyalty to the company. However, unlike Dorothy Lane, which mails its customer reward certificates, Big Y saves both time and the mailing cost by giving a customer her reward while she is checking out.

Another fascinating feature of Big Y's token program is that each month the company has a sweepstake featuring very attractive prizes such as a Chevy pickup truck, a Jeep Wrangler, a 50-inch television set, or various cruises. Each winner is alerted as she presents her *Express Savings Club* card. Alarm bells start ringing, strobe lights flash, and the manager dashes to the appropriate checkout to tell the surprised and delighted customer that she has just won a fabulous prize. What excitement! What publicity! Big Y is, like Superquinn, another company that believes in having fun.

A sister program to the tokens program is what manufacturers call Big Y's "pog" (ie, milk-top like) program. Every week, cashiers give qualified customers, upon prompting by a screen message, a 9" x 4" heavy cardboard sheet containing six round, push-out, pog-type tokens. Manufacturers participate with Big Y in this pog program, targeting customers with free or heavily discounted product offers (eg, a 20 oz can of free Dole Pineapple or $1.00 off a half gallon of Friendly's Ice Cream). The goal?—To build sales. Manufacturers love the pog program, not just because the pogs go to the "right customers" but, just as important, there are no mailing costs. And Big Y loves it too, as it gives relevant offers only to relevant customers.

Given Big Y's crazy price promotions and its in-store colored tokens and pog sheets, it should come as no surprise that the shoppers in Massachusetts and Connecticut love Big Y. Nor should it be surprising that Big Y has one of the highest percentages of sales captured on a loyalty card anywhere in the world. *Behavior follows rewards.*

WITH A LITTLE HELP FROM ITS FRIEND: TECHNOLOGY

Big Y is an outstanding example of a company that has married technology with marketing. It uses its front-end systems for a number of marketing, communication, and operational purposes:

* To identify and manage customer markdowns (no card-holder can buy more than five units of any item at the advertised price at any store during the promotional week).

❖ To communicate with selected customers via a customer message screen as her order is being processed.

❖ To identify sweepstakes winners, with fanfare, at the checkout (Big Y was the first supermarket chain in the US ever to have a million-dollar sweepstakes).

❖ To allocate coupons based on spending—from time to time, Big Y runs special manufacturer coupon redemption programs in which the number of coupons allocated is based upon the customer's spending. For example, one triple coupon can be redeemed for every $20 of accumulated spending by the customer.

❖ To run unique promotions. For example, one Easter, Big Y offered a free spiral ham to customers who bought any combination of fifteen General Mills' products that were listed on the front page of the weekly ad. They were well displayed, and included such items as popcorn, Betty Crocker products, and cereals.

THE EDUCATION EDGE

Even though the *Express Savings Club* card is based on prices, Big Y is also extremely well known for its points-based *Education Express* program, which is featured every couple of years. Since 1994 Big Y has raised millions of dollars for computers, books, sports equipment, etc, for local schools.

The *Education Express* program is very simple. *Express Savings Club* cardholders sign up, indicating the school to which they wish to donate the points they earn. Then, each time a customer buys a specially marked *Education Express* item, the school earns the points indicated on the shelf tag. These *Education Express* items are featured in Big Y's weekly ad, in special brochures, and in special in-store displays. Manufacturers heavily support this program, significantly increasing the point value on the featured items.

At regular intervals, each school is advised of its accrued points balance. At the program's end, the points can be redeemed for a wide variety of educational needs featured both in a school-needs catalog and on a special website. Not only are these programs great for the schools, they also build loyalty towards Big Y. And it is accomplished effortlessly, thanks to the interlocking of technology and the *Express Savings Club*.

THE HOMEWORK HELP LINE

Big Y is also involved in another landmark education program that helps build goodwill towards the company. Its *Homework Help Line* offers free homework assistance to any student anywhere in Massachusetts and Connecticut between 4 and 7 pm, Monday through Thursday, every school week. Students can call and talk to an actual teacher on subjects ranging from Arithmetic to Zoology. The role of the teacher is to talk through the concepts on the homework problem, but never to give the answers. Hundreds of calls are received and answered every evening.

As a result, many homes in the area feature Big Y magnets on their refrigerators with the Homework Help Line 800-telephone number. Imagine, year-round, a loyalty-generating reminder in one of the most frequented locations in a customer's home. It's no surprise that this program, although not directly related to their *Express Club Card* program, is probably just as well known.

It reminds us once again that loyalty building is not the exclusive domain of a loyalty card. Loyalty is built on myriad touchpoints—the contacts and interactions—customers have with a company.

A GREAT PIONEER

I consider Big Y to be one of the great pioneers in loyalty card marketing: highly promotional with eye-catching offers, yet at the same time, it has a bias towards rewarding its Best Customers. This company introduced key ring cards to the northeastern United States. It was the pioneer of million dollar sweepstakes among US food retailers. Big Y is a pioneer with both its *Education Express* program and its Homework Help Line. And it's a pioneer in low-cost, customer-related communications and technology.

Big Y has used freeway billboards to remind customers of its leadership in loyalty card marketing. When a major competitor launched its card program three years after Big Y's program had been established, Big Y's billboards responded with: "Often imitated. But never equaled!"

On a recent visit to the *Express Savings Card* section of the Big-Y website, I saw a message that was firmly based upon the foundations it laid in 1991:

- ❖ Lost key returns
- ❖ Free membership
- ❖ Check cashing privileges
- ❖ No minimum purchases necessary
- ❖ Double manufacturers coupons up to 99 cents
- ❖ Automatically entered to win when you use the card
- ❖ Show your card and save at local businesses and events

Big Y's pioneering efforts in the market place are also echoed behind the scenes. Not only is the company a world-class marketer, it is among the leaders in using its customer information. For example, a Big Y category manager not only looks at how the average customer shops his category, he also quantifies the behavior of the company's Best Customers in his category. As a result of this and similar analysis, the company has been able to regain such customers in categories where they had stopped shopping.

Big Y goes even further, analyzing its Best Customer spending profiles by individual store and then tweaking each store's product mix accordingly. It is a company that realizes that customer information should not be left lying in the marketing department!

THE BOTTOM LINE

I admire Big Y's marketing savvy, its analytical ability, its technical superiority, its simplicity and consistency, its audaciousness, and its committed, focused leadership. Big Y is a large retailer that, because it is a private company, has slipped under the radar screens of most observers. It's a company that just goes about its work promoting like crazy and building the loyalty of its Best Customers. Big Y navigates the shoals of a highly competitive marketplace by plumbing the information from its extensive customer database.

A RETAILER'S VIEW

Let's learn how Big Y views its loyalty card program. Dan Lescoe, Big Y's senior vice president of merchandising and marketing, who has had responsibility for the *Express Savings Club* from its earliest days, was asked the same two loyalty questions as before.

Dan, what's your bottom line on the Express Savings Card?

"The Express Savings Card gives us a separate identity as a company. It helps differentiate us—and build our unique brand. Internally, we have always treated our card program as a religion and all marketing decisions revolve around it. Whenever any executive, no matter what his area of responsibility, thinks of changing something, he first asks: How will it affect the card program? The card is such a flexible tool, allowing us to stay at the cutting edge with all sorts of new ideas. Not only that, the information it provides has made us all so much smarter and more astute as business people. Our card program has not only been a really great sales builder, but it has also provided us with huge cost savings."

Why, then, don't all retailers have a loyalty card program?

"There are probably two main reasons. First, many retailers still think traditionally and don't see how they can benefit from a card program. Second, many have no idea of the value of the data generated—it really is a goldmine!"

BEST CUSTOMER MARKETING

Chapter **8**

If you reward everyone, there will not be enough to go around, so you offer a reward to one in order to encourage everyone.
... Sun Tzu, *The Art of War* (written over 2400 years ago)

Fish where the fish are, and if possible, where the big fish are.
... Garth Hallberg, *All Consumers Are Not Created Equal*

Having a Best Customer marketing strategy is common sense—but not common practice. It simply means that we give the greatest attention to those customers who provide us with the majority of our sales and profits. It's a classic segmentation strategy with one goal: increase the number of high-spending Best Customers per store.

The reasoning is elementary. As a general rule, our Best Customers:

* Spend the most each year
* Have the lowest defection rates
* Visit us most frequently each month
* Buy items with a higher average price
* Buy higher gross margin percentage items
* Buy from more departments and categories

❖ Have lower processing costs (eg, larger order sizes, fewer questions about where to find items, fewer losses from bad checks)

As a result, Best Customers have the highest lifetime value. Therefore, if we wish to optimize our short and long term profits, we should do everything possible to:

❖ Retain our high-spending customers at their current spending levels, and

❖ Develop programs that will increase their numbers

As mentioned before, this goes beyond card-related activities; it involves every facet of customer contact.

From a cost viewpoint, concentrating one's focus in favor of higher-spending customers also makes sense. Almost without exception, the best returns on targeted offers come from our higher spenders. This is because they are already favorably inclined towards us and any special offer we make is simply a matter of them increasing their spending a notch or two. In contrast, offers to low-spending customers to encourage them to become regular customers are, usually, very expensive because they require a significant change in these customers' shopping habits. (They, obviously, are currently doing their primary shopping elsewhere.) Hence the typical negative returns to retailers when they target the bottom section of their database.

WHO ARE BEST CUSTOMERS?

Definitions of Best Customers vary. Ideally, they should be defined as our highest spending, highest profit-producing customers. In practice many retailers reduce this to just the highest spenders as they don't have the ability to accurately calculate the profitability of each customer.

Best Customers are our primary shoppers and typically comprise the top 12% to 25% of our customers and account for 40% to 65% of our sales. Among US food retailers, they are usually defined as those who spend over $650 in a 13-week quarter, ie, those who spend, each week, an average of $50 or more. Using the DROP'N classification described in Chapter 3, Best Customers are our Diamonds and Rubies.

For international comparisons, the current average selling price per item among US food retailers is approximately $2.00. Therefore a Best Customer buys, on average, 25 or more items per week. This compares with the average order size for all transactions of $20 (ie, 10 items).

Some businesses have definition complications because of the mix of their business. For example, a hypermarket sells both food and high-priced general merchandise (refrigerators, televisions, etc). By using a straight spending qualification, a customer who is typically a low-spender could be a Best Customer one quarter because she happened to buy a refrigerator. Because of such erratic spending fluctuations, there is a strong case for such companies to base their Best Customer threshold purely on their customers' regular food purchases.

Another approach to classifying Best Customers was used by Sears when it introduced its Best Customer program in the early 1990s. Sears used a set of four criteria: *a pre-qualification period* (having been a member of its Club for at least a year); *shopping breadth* (bought from a minimum number of departments during the year); *frequency* (shopped a minimum number of times); and *spending* (exceeded a spending threshold during the year).

My experience suggests that the best approach is to keep it simple: use total spending as the qualifier for the Best Customer program and offer a basic set of benefits and rewards. Then, behind the scenes, give unannounced rewards and benefits that vary with the value and needs of your various Best Customer sub-segments. In this way, both bipolar and multi-department shopping can be accommodated as can, say, an allowance for the length of time a customer has been shopping with you.

A TWO-LEVEL BEST CUSTOMER PROGRAM

Palais Royal is a company with such a two-tier Best Customer reward program. Because of their wider range of products and services, department stores have an easier task than food retailers in designing such reward packages for their Best Customers. This Houston, Texas-based retailer offers a brochure to customers explaining the benefits available to its two highest-spending segments (Figure 21).

In addition to the announced benefits, the company has an unannounced range of benefits that vary by Best Customer subgroups. These include advance notice of special sales; mailings that offer 25% off any single item; private sales; special double-point and triple-point events; one-day additional 10% off offers; scratch-and-win cards that give from 10% to 100% off any purchase; and individualized customer gifts.

The Palais Royal program is based on how much a customer spends in a calendar year as recorded on her proprietary credit card, with the benefits available throughout the following year. As we see from Palais Royal's benefit package, it's not hard to be creative when it comes to paying special attention to those few customers who provide the majority of the company's sales and profits.

The Palais Royal V.I.P. Charge Card Gives You
Unique Rewards and Privileges

No other retail card offers so much, and with no annual fee! This unique program, with all its benefits and privileges, is yours when you have earned at least 750 VIP Points, during the course of any single year. Each dollar you charge on your Palais Royal account gives you one VIP Point.

To secure VIP status, earn at least 750 VIP Points annually, while maintaining regular account payments. It's just one more reason for shopping at Palais Royal.

V.I. P. Gold

Earn 1,000 or more Palais Royal VIP points annually and you get:
Twice-A-Year Additional 20% Savings for VIPs Only
Free Gift Wrap Service
Emergency Check Cashing Up To $200
Free Credit Card Registration
Free Date Reminder Service
Free Cosmetic Makeovers
Choose Your Own Billing Date
50% Off Fur Storage (One fur per VIP account)
25% Off All Alteration Charges
Special Vacation Giveaway Contest
Free Address Change Notification Service
Access To The President's Service Committee
Free 24-hour Message Service
Free Travel Reservation Service
Free Valuable Document Registration
Free Notary Public Service

V.I.P. Silver

Earn 750 or more Palais Royal VIP points annually and you get:
Twice-A-Year Additional 15% Savings for VIPs Only
50% Off Gift Wrap Service
Free Address Change Notification Service
Access to the President's Service Committee
Free Travel Reservation Service
Free Valuable Document Registration
Free Notary Public Service

FIGURE 21: PALAIS ROYAL BEST CUSTOMER BENEFITS

WHAT WE KNOW ABOUT BEST CUSTOMERS

One of the great benefits of a loyalty card program is that we can now gain much deeper insights into the behavior of our different customer groups. The curtain of comprehension parts as we delve into our database.

Many businesses find that the very highest spenders (the top 1% to 3% of customers) often place a greater value on personal recognition and rewards than on price reductions. The nature and value of these are, of course, retailer-specific. For high-end retailer Neiman Marcus, one highly valued privilege among their very top (and very high-spending) customers has been lunch with the store manager followed by a private fashion show for the customer and a few friends. For other retailers whose top customer spending is not as stratospheric as at Neiman Marcus, a series of less expensive expressions, such as chocolates or floral gifts, are more appropriate.

By studying the markdown percentages among Best Customers and looking at their response rates to targeted promotional offers, we find that the majority of Best Customers are, indeed, price sensitive in varying degrees. We need to be aware of these differences and the corresponding levels of profitability as we structure additional offers for them. In structuring a Best Customer package, our goal should be to have maximum flexibility. This is to allow us to readily individualize the rewards and benefits according to the specific needs of individual stores and our ever-changing competitive conditions. The fewer publicly announced hard benefits we offer to Best Customers, the lower will be our fixed-cost commitment and the greater will be our flexibility.

My most surprising discovery when first exposed to Best Customer shopping behavior was the volatility of their spending. Best Customers are, without question, loyal—they have the lowest defection rate of any customer segment—but they aren't *consistently* high spenders, as seen in Tables 22 and 23. These tables show two different approaches to analyzing

Best Customer behavior at two distinctly different companies. What they reveal, however, is common.

Table 22, *Customer Activity from One Quarter to the Next,* shows the spending levels of one company's Pre-Existing Active Customers (PEAs) during two consecutive quarters. It shows a lot of customer churn. With results reminiscent of what we saw in Chapter 2, we see that for every 1,000 Pre-Existing Active Customers in this chain:

❖ Customer defections were lowest among Best Customers (0.9%) and highest among the lowest spenders, the Pearls (16.8%) (col. g, rows 1 & 3).

❖ Among the 232 Best Customers (over $50 per week) who returned the following quarter, 186 (or 80%) spent at the same level, while a significant 17% dropped one spending level to Opals ($25-50 per week), and 3% dropped to the bottom spending Pearls level (<$25 per week) (row 5, b & f-h).

❖ Among the 213 Opals who continued shopping in the following quarter, a significant 17% moved up to the Best Customer group but a more significant 28% dropped to the lowest spending group (row 6, f & h). This tells us that the mid-spending group is more likely to decrease spending than to increase it and reminds us of the sales-building challenge we have with that group.

❖ Of the returnees among the Pearls—the largest and lowest spending customer group—most (86%) remained as low spenders (row 7, h). Only 2% of the returnees became Best Customers, reminding us of the difficulty of trying to significantly change the behavior of our lowest spending customer group.

	(a)	(b)	(c)	(d)	(e)	(f)	(g)	(h)
	Base Quarter		Base Qtr.	Following Qtr.			% of	
	Customer Segment	Avg. SPW	# HH #	Inactive #	Returned #	Tot.HHs (=col.c)	Cust. Segment Inactive	Return
1	Best Cust.	>$50	234	2	**232**	23.4%	0.9%	99.1%
2	Opals	$25-50	218	5	**213**	21.8%	2.3%	97.7%
3	Pearls	<$25	548	92	**456**	54.8%	16.8%	83.2%
4	Total		1,000	99	**901**	100.0%	9.9%	90.1%

Spending Levels of Those Returning in the Following Quarter

	Customer Segment	BC >$50	Opals $25-50	Pearls <$25	Returned #	% of Segment		
						BC	Opals	Pearls
5	Best Cust.	186	39	7	**232**	80%	17%	3%
6	Opals	37	116	60	**213**	17%	55%	28%
7	Pearls	7	56	393	**456**	2%	12%	86%
8	Total	230	211	460	**901**	26%	23%	51%
9	Original Base	234	218	548	1,000			
10	Better (Worse)	(4)	(7)	(88)	(99)			
11	B(W)%	(2)%	(3)%	(16)%	(10)%			

How to Read

Row 1: In the Base Qtr., there were 234 Best Customers. Of these, 2 (or 0.9%) didn't return the following Qtr., while 232 (99.1%) did.

Row 5: Of the 232 BCs who returned, 186 (80%) stayed at that spending level, while 39 (17%) dropped to Opals and 7 (3%) dropped to Pearls.

TABLE 22: CUSTOMER ACTIVITY FROM ONE QUARTER TO THE NEXT

		(a)	(b)	(c)	(d)	(e)	(f)	(g)	(h)

Later Spending Levels of Best Customer Households

		SPW	Q1 Y1 Q	Q2Y1 Q + 1	Q3Y1 Q + 2	Q4Y1 Q + 3	Q1Y2 Q + 4	Q2Y2 Q + 5	Q3Y2 Q + 6
1	BC	>$50	1,000	708	714	794	641	650	583
2	O	$25-$50		203	213	135	142	147	154
3	P	<$25		28	66	54	61	76	84
4		Inactive		61	7	17	156	127	179
5		Total	1,000	1,000	1,000	1,000	1,000	1,000	1,000

Results Per 1,000 BCs

Above Expressed as % of Base 1,000 Households

		SPW	Q	Q + 1	Q + 2	Q + 3	Q + 4	Q + 5	Q + 6
6	BC	<$50	100%	71%	71%	79%	64%	65%	58%
7	O	$25-$50		20%	21%	14%	14%	15%	15%
8	P	<$25		3%	7%	5%	6%	8%	8%
9		Inactive		6%	1%	2%	16%	13%	18%
10		Key Cust %		91%	92%	93%	78%	80%	73%
11		Active %		94%	99%	98%	84%	87%	82%

BC = Best Customers ($50+ per week); O = Opals ($25-50); P = Pearls (<$25).

Key Customers = customers spending $25+ per week (ie, rows 1 & 2; 6 & 7).

TABLE 23: BEST CUSTOMERS' SUBSEQUENT BEHAVIOR BY QUARTER

❖ The net effect, after allowing both for customers becoming inactive and changes in spending levels in the following quarter, was a net loss of 2% in the number of Best Customers from the preceding quarter, a loss of 3% from the Opals base, and a 16% loss from the Pearls base (row 11). In total, the company suffered a loss of 10% of their Pre-Existing Active Customer base (row 11, e). We always hope that this loss will be offset by new customers.

The changes in this table highlight the degree of customer volatility, including Key Customers, Best Customers, and Opals.

Table 23 provides us with a wider perspective of Best Customer spending. It shows, at another retailer, their behavior over six subsequent quarters. For every 1,000 Best Customer households in Quarter 1 Year 1, we see that:

❖ Best Customers did not consistently stay at that high-spending level over time. Over the subsequent six quarters, the percentage maintaining that spending level ranged from 58% to 79% (the Christmas quarter) (row 6). In other words, in each subsequent quarter, 21% to 42% of the Best Customers fell below the $50 per week spending threshold. Fortunately, most dropped only one level, to Opal ($25-50 per week) (rows 2 and 7).

❖ Best Customers who dropped to the lowest spending level, Pearls (under $25 per week), never accounted for more than 8% of the base (row 8). This suggests that when Best Customers do shop, most spend reasonably well.

❖ There is surprising volatility in the Best Customer quarterly inactivity, ranging from 1% to 18% in the subsequent six quarters (row 9). Yes, some customers do move to locations where we don't have stores and many go on vacation; even so, it's hard to imagine why 18% of this company's Best Customers didn't shop at any time during one consecutive 13-week period, unless there was unhappiness with some element of the company's basic offer of service, friendliness, quality, or price.

New helpful measurement tools

Drawing from these new insights on Best Customers, some very helpful customer measures of our business success have been developed, including our:

* *Best Customer Decline Rate:* the percentage of Best Customers who fall below the Best Customer threshold

* *Retention Rate as Key Customers:* the percentage of customers who spent above the Key Customer threshold ($25 per week) both last year and again this year

The former is important because any significant change in our Best Customers total means unhappiness in our core constituency and needs to be identified and corrected immediately. The latter is important because it includes not just our Best Customers still spending above the threshold, but many who have slipped just below it, together with those who have the highest potential to move up to Best Customer status. Our Key Customers comprise, in effect, our regular customers; the more of them we can retain at that level, the greater our sales will be.

Another valuable measure is our *Best Customer Weekly Return Rate* (Table 24). Rather than wait until the end of each quarter to see how many Best Customers we have compared to last year, this report allows us to measure our progress weekly.

The average number of Best Customers per store in the previous quarter (2,860) is shown at the top right of the report. Then, recorded each week during the current quarter is the number of Best Customers from last quarter that returned to shop (regardless of how much they spent in the week).

Store: Greenville Plaza	Results For Qtr. 1		Best Customers in Previous Qtr.			2,860
(a)	(b)	(c)	(d)	(e)	(f)	(g)
Week.. W/E..	Week 1 6-Jan	Week 2 13-Jan	Week 3 20-Jan	Week 4 27 Jan	etc. thru >	Week 13 31-Mar
Return Rate, By Week						
1 BCs Who Returned to Shop	2,266	2,258	2,315	2,324		
2 Return Rate (%)	79.2%	79.0%	80.9%	81.3%		
3 Better (Worse)than LY pp	(3.6)%	(0.2)%	0.4%	(3.5)%		
Return Rate, QTD						
4 BCs Who Returned to Shop	2,266	2,262	2,280	2,291		
5 Return Rate (%)	79.2%	79.1%	79.7%	80.1%		
6 Better (Worse) than Ly pp	(3.6)%	(2.0)%	0.1%	(0.5)%		

pp = percentage points

TABLE 24: BEST CUSTOMER WEEKLY RETURN RATE REPORT

For example, in week 4 we see that 2,324 of last quarter's Best Customers returned, ie, 81.3% of 2,860 (rows 1-2, col. e). This was a 3.5% lower return rate than last year's 84.8% (row 3, col. e).

For the first four weeks, the average number of returnees per week was 2,291 ([2266+2258+2315+2324] ÷ 4 = 2291), an average rate of 80.1%, down 0.5% from the same period last year (rows 4-6, col. e).

This weekly report is helpful because, typically, there is a correlation between the better or worse percentage in rows 3 and 6 with the year-to-year net change in Best Customer numbers at the end of the quarter. Thus, using this weekly measure can prompt corrective action whenever there are material changes from last year.

DOES A BEST CUSTOMER FOCUS WORK IN PRACTICE?

Yes. In our work we have found a direct correlation between the number of Best Customers and a company's sales and profits over time. This, of course, is intuitively obvious: if we can encourage an increasing number of high-spending customers to choose us as their primary store, then we are doing many things right (service, quality, price, assortment, etc). That package of "right things" flows over and appeals to a widening number of lower spending customers. Result: both our Best Customer numbers increase and our *Retention Rate as Key Customers* measurement improves, giving us increased sales and profits.

Let's look at the year-to-year results of one leading loyalty marketer to illustrate what can happen when Best Customers become central to the company's marketing efforts. In Table 25, we see a company that has raised the bar on itself by increasing its Best Customer spending threshold from the typical $50 per week to $60 per week, which explains its lower than usual share of Best Customers.

The company's average weekly store sales were $338,616, up 10.2% over the preceding year (row 3). Of this total, 87.4% were cardholder sales, at $295,950, up only 9.1% (row 8) because of a small decline (0.9%, row 4) in the sales captured on the card.

Driving the store's strong average sales gain was a huge 16.1% increase in the number of Best Customers per store (row 9), compared to an overall increase in cardholders of 4.5% (row 12). This 16.1% jump, combined with a 3.9% increase in average spending per week (row 13) yielded a 20.7% increase in Best Customer sales per trading week (row 5). By focusing on satisfying its core customer constituency, this company pushed sales (and also profits, which are not shown in this table) to new heights.

Averages Per Store		Quarter 2		
Description		**TY**	**LY**	**Chg**
1	Spending Per Visit: Total Transactions	$	21.41	19.92	7.5%
2	Total Transactions PTW	$	15,816	15,421	2.6%
3	Total Reported Sales PTW	$	**338,616**	**307,209**	**10.2%**
4	Card/Total Sales	%	87.4%	88.3%	(0.9)%
5	Best Customers	$	122,407	101,433	20.7%
6	Potential Best	$	169,768	166,121	2.2%
7	New	$	3,775	3,712	1.7%
8	**Card Sales Per Trading Week (SPTW)**	$	**295,950**	**271,266**	**9.1%**
9	Best Customers	#	1,478	1,273	16.1%
10	Potential Best	#	8,421	8,161	3.2%
11	New	#	312	338	(7.7)%
12	**Number of Active Cardholders**	#	**10,211**	**9,772**	**4.5%**
13	Best Customers	$	82.81	79.69	3.9%
14	Potential Best	$	20.16	20.36	(1.0)%
15	New	$	12.12	10.98	10.4%
16	**Cardholder Spending Per Week (SPW)**	$	**28.98**	**27.76**	**4.4%**

TABLE 25: RESULTS OF A STRONG BEST CUSTOMER PROGRAM

Are all its results perfect? No. They never are, not at any company. There was a slight decline in sales captured on the card; the Potential Best Customers results weren't in the same growth class as the Best Customers (because many moved up to the higher group); and there were 26 fewer new customers per week in Quarter 2 this year than last year (row 11). But these minor blemishes are all correctable. The overall picture is what a truly customer-centric organization can accomplish when it has the right balance of priorities and a good set of measurements to monitor its progress.

CASE STUDIES

THE HARRIS TEETER BEST CUSTOMER APPROACH

There are many ways to focus on and recognize Best Customers. Last year, a neighbor told me she had just received from Harris Teeter, a Charlotte, NC-based food retailer, a package of three different pasta items and one of Parmesan cheese. Accompanying the surprise package was a letter indicating that she was one of its best customers and invited her to try these special private label items and then to complete and return an enclosed comment card.

The experience had a very positive impact on her. She had been recognized as an important customer and she found these new products to be of excellent quality. To the company, it was another touchpoint with a valuable customer, introducing her to products available only in its stores, thereby adding another differentiation factor. Alone, such an action probably had no great impact. But as part of an overall plan of regularly touching base with Best Customers in diverse ways, it creates a powerful message.

My neighbor's experience is part of Harris Teeter's total marketing plan, which has a heavy Best Customer bias. Throughout the whole year, the company runs continuity programs that reward frequency and spending. Its recent Easter promotion was typical: *Make a purchase of at least $35 purchase in 12 out of the next 13 weeks and receive a $40.00 Harris Teeter Gift Card, or make one purchase in 10 of the next 13 weeks and receive a $25.00 Harris Teeter Gift Card.* Each time a customer spent at least $35 in a transaction, an acknowledgement certificate was printed at the checkout.

The company recognizes that frequency creates and reinforces habits, as well as drives spending. Harris Teeter realizes that customers who participate in its continuity programs, while not spending all their food budgets with the company, will be spending a lot more than the $35 spending requirement. The threshold is also low enough to appeal to that group of customers, the Opals, who have the potential to qualify for its $50 per week Best Customers group.

As an aside here, what might puzzle some readers is why Harris Teeter, with its sophisticated point-of-sale technology, issues a customer a slip of paper for her to save to record her progress, when it could be done so simply with a few key strokes by a computer operator. What Harris Teeter has found, along with so many other loyalty marketers around the world, is that if too much is done automatically for customers they overlook it or forget about it. They either don't appreciate or are unaware what the company is doing for them. I have seen companies call customers and tell them they have won a car in their sweepstakes with the surprised customers responding they were unaware they were even entered! This ignorance occurred because customer names were automatically entered each time they shopped. Similar experiences have occurred with the automatic issuance of double points to customers. "Out of sight, out of mind" as the old expression goes. So Harris Teeter issues the paper "reminders" to customers reflecting what most loyalty marketers have discovered: *High tech doesn't replace high touch.*

This customer sensitivity is common at Harris Teeter. For example, to appeal to those Best Customers who are price conscious yet, at the same time, to ensure that the other Best Customers don't feel left out, Harris Teeter frequently mails all Best Customers various *opt-in offers* such as: *Redeem the enclosed coupon for $10 off a $50 order next week and you'll receive another to redeem the following week* (which is repeated again, for four weeks). Only those opting into the program in the initial week are eligible.

Besides its on-going $35 per-week frequency reward programs, Harris Teeter offers other programs that appeal to its higher-spending customer segments, such as its Baby Club and School Donations programs. The company even e-mails selected customers with notification of upcoming three-day sales.

At the same time, Harris Teeter carefully monitors the behavior of its Best Customers, including identifying those customers whose spending has dropped precipitously or who have stopped shopping. To these, the company reaches out to find out why and to encourage them to return. One such letter recently sent by the company's president included the following:

> Our records indicate that you have decreased your shopping or stopped shopping at Harris Teeter and this concerns us. Did something happen that we need to address? Please let us know by filling out the attached satisfaction survey and returning it as soon as possible. At Harris Teeter, we value your opinion. If you need to contact us immediately, please call our Customer Relations Department at 1-800-432-6111 and tell our customer service representative you received this mailing.
>
> As an invitation to come back, please accept the attached $5-off coupons for use over the next four weeks.

Harris Teeter understands the critical value of its Best Customers. As Kevin Crainer, director of VIC marketing at Harris Teeter, recently told me: "A major portion of our CRM strategy is based on rewarding our Best Customers and building their number, which has continued to increase as a result of our program focusing on rewarding consistent higher spending."

A-Coop: A Simple But Excellent Program

In this book there are many examples of how different loyalty leaders have focused on their Best Customer segment with varying levels of sophistication. But a Best Customer strategy can also be elegantly simple, as I learned when visiting A-Coop, an independent, high-volume food retailer in Shirane, a rural town about 100 kilometers from Tokyo. Toshiro Kanemaru, the manager and conceptualizer of its program, explained how it works.

A-Coop's loyalty program is points-based. For every ¥100 spent, a cardholder is credited with 1.5 points. To join, there is a one-time sign-up fee of ¥500 (approximately US$5). Only one bar-coded card is issued per member, allowing the cardholder to be in complete control of her points and avoiding conflicts sometimes seen when several cardholders have access to the points balance in a household account. The customer must always present her card to earn her points. If she forgets it, she receives no points. Should she lose her card, there is a ¥200 replacement fee.

Despite these minor restrictions, A-Coop's program attracts strong usage and loyalty, with members generating over 80% of total sales. Since 1996, when its loyalty card program was relaunched, the company has enjoyed strong growth each year. Why?

Prior to its program relaunch, A-Coop, like many Japanese food retailers, distributed three circulars every week. After its relaunch, the circulars were eliminated. It doesn't have two-tier prices associated with its card, but it does offer very aggressive prices on selected items for several months at a time. Using an in-store hot sheet, it offers attractive daily and weekly specials. And, occasionally, A-Coop will offer bonus points on various products.

So how does a simple points program help A-Coop? By focusing on a few critical loyalty-building elements.

The company offers quintuple points on the 5th, 15th, and 25th of every month. This is a points-based alternative to Big Y's *Buy One Get Two Free* price promotions discussed in the previous chapter, and has a similar effect. Customer traffic and sales jump dramatically on these days at A-Coop, but without the cost of circular advertising, price markdowns, or labor-intensive special displays, and without any overstocks of unsold promotional merchandise. In fact, what typically happens, as you might expect, is that customers stock up on higher-priced, higher-margin items, such as rice and alcohol, on these days. What a simple, non-disruptive magnet! Every ten days, customers are drawn to the store where, in their own best interests, they shop heavily.

Next to the customer service center is the store's single points kiosk. At any time, customers can check their current points balance or trigger a "P" certificate in exchange for 1,000 accumulated points. "P" certificates, which have a nominal face value of ¥1,000 (US$10), can be used as payment towards any purchase during the year or they may be used in one of two other special ways.

At regular intervals during the year, cardholders can enter a lottery to participate in seven or eight special events that A-Coop organizes. The annual events include a day trip to Tokyo Disneyland, a big league baseball game in Tokyo, gift certificates for special nearby restaurants and popular toys at extremely low prices at Christmas. The events are listed in the store with reminders in the store's weekly hot sheet. Because of the great value involved, availability is limited (eg, 100 passes to Disneyland) and there is a price, expressed in "P" certificates, to the winners. A customer completes an application for the event of her choice, indicating the number of tickets (up to six) that she would like. For example, the Disneyland trip may require one "P" certificate per attendee while the baseball game may require two per attendee. Winners are drawn from the applicants and notified.

The second special use of points is A-Coop's annual major points redemption day. On a designated day early in December, each "P" certificate redeemed has a value 50% greater than on the other 364 days. This redemption day is one of the busiest of the year for A-Coop. To customers, the day is a type of cost-free Christmas club as they stock up for the holiday season using their unused accumulated points.

A-Coop also pays a great deal more attention to the customer information generated by its card program than I currently see among most other Japanese retailers. Each month, management carefully studies an impressively detailed, double-sized sheet of customer statistics. They review cardholder activity—and inactivity—and compare the month's results with each of the preceding 13 months. They check to see whether their number of Best Customers is continuing to increase and if their new cardholder application numbers are holding up. This report of 20 key customer measures, covering each of the past 13 months, is an integral part of the company's operating performance review and plays a key role in A-Coop's success as a retailer.

Why do I consider this program to be a noteworthy example of a Best Customer program? First, because A-Coop has built a solid base of loyalty-generating basics apart from its loyalty card program: its store is attractive, well lit, and well merchandised, with good service, good quality, and it has competitive prices. Second, because its program, albeit simple, rewards its regular, high-spending customers the most. These customers are the ones who, because of their regularity and promotional knowledge, take most advantage of the quintuple points days. They are the ones who, because of their accumulated points balances, are best able to take advantage of the special event offers and the early December redemption promotion. All of these elements interplay with one other and keep those customers coming back.

Finally, A-Coop carefully monitors its progress with customers. It has mainlined its key customer statistics into the core of its business process and uses these metrics to help guide the company in developing an even better customer shopping experience.

In summary, A-Coop epitomizes the essence of the Second Act. Its basics (quality, variety, cleanliness, service) are first class; it has a marketing bias in favor of its Best Customers; and, every month, it carefully tracks its customer progress against both planned and past performance. It has developed an outstanding closed-loop system.

THE INFORMATION PARADOX

The typical loyalty card program seeks to capture a high share of sales so that higher-spending customers can be identified and receive concentrated attention while less emphasis is given to the other customers. The *information paradox* is that we gather data from a large number of customers yet focus only on the minority that drives our business.

An increasing number of retailers are now wondering how they can short-circuit this process by introducing an entrance filter to their program that, while attractive to high-spending Best Customers, is unattractive to low spenders. This would then provide only the data of those customers they wish to focus on, thereby saving unnecessary costs.

Diverse companies have already successfully taken this approach. One of the best known is the Neiman Marcus InCircle® program. When the program was launched in 1984, the only credit card accepted by the company was Neiman Marcus' own proprietary card, accounting for the vast majority of its sales. Thus, to go into its credit card base and advise customers that they were members of their InCircle® program (spending $3,000+ per year) was easy. Members didn't even need a separate card.

The company then showered lavish, tiered rewards upon this critical group. It introduced a range of exclusive special events, such as double-point Private Shopping Parties for its Best Customers. Further, individualized recognition was given to each InCircle® member on the day before, the day of, or the day after the member's birthday, with double points earned on which ever of those three days was chosen by the customer.

A few years later, in response to those customers who didn't meet the InCircle® spending qualification but sought special recognition by the company, a new card, Neiman Marcus Plus (since renamed the Neiman Marcus Gold Card) was launched. To join and be eligible for special recognition and benefits (at a lower level than the InCircle® program), customers paid a $50 entrance fee. This was, of course, an excellent filter, allowing potential Best Customers to identify themselves.

Other companies use an annual membership fee as the self-identifier of their Best Customers. For example, the Paris-based Sofetil hotel chain has two self-qualification levels: its Exclusive Business Card (US$190 annual fee) and its Exclusive Card (US$70 annual fee). Each program has an array of benefits, such as a VIP Welcome, discounts, complimentary stays, and guaranteed room availability. Obviously, only regular guests would be interested in the Exclusive Card program and only very frequent guests would be interested in the Exclusive Business program. The two fees act as very effective Best Customer entrance filters.

Some years ago, WaldenBooks launched a card program with an annual fee of $10, entitling members to a 10% discount along with other benefits. The base reward package meant that only customers who spent over $100 annually would be interested in the program. The benefit to WaldenBooks was a much clearer understanding of the buying habits of its better customers.

In 2001, Barnes & Noble took a narrower approach when it launched its loyalty card program. Its annual membership fee is $25, meaning that only those who expect to spend over $250 with Barnes & Noble in a year should contemplate joining the program if they wish to break even with the 10% membership discount. With the higher fee, its approach is even more refined than WaldenBooks in encouraging Best Customers to identify themselves. One assumes that Barnes & Noble, armed with information on this key reading segment, will, among other actions, effect a series of targeted programs to take a larger share of these customers' book-buying budgets.

It's probable that the heavy book-buying customers who enroll also buy books on the Internet from Amazon.com.

Therefore, the discount offered to cardholders when they order from Barnes&Noble.com is likely to have some effect on the two companies' relative market shares.

The first food retailer to introduce a fee-based loyalty card program aimed at its Best Customers was Larry's Markets, of Bellevue, Washington. This regional operator of large, upscale supermarkets invites customers to join its Epicurean Association. As its website explains, a $40 annual fee gives members a variety of benefits, including a 15% discount on general wine purchases as well as sealed-case pricing at 10% over cost. Members receive discounts on selected "Epicurean" food products and culinary tools, and for exclusive wine and food events, classes, and tastings. In addition, members receive priority notice regarding new product releases, special offers and sale events. They also receive a subscription to the *Epicurean,* its monthly food and wine newsletter (which includes special price offers available to members only).

Given the annual fee, Larry's has found that, as expected, only its high spenders (ie, Best Customers) identify themselves. Using this information, special relationship, retention, and sales-building programs have been developed to maximize the potential of this critical group.

In the coming years, I expect that we will see many more programs like that of Larry's and Barnes & Noble that charge an annual fee, short-circuiting the whole information gathering process. Such is mutually satisfactory to both customer and retailer. A customer doesn't wish to be forced to carry a card for almost every retailer at which she shops; she wants to carry them only for those that provide her primary needs in each sector. Similarly, a retailer doesn't wish to spend a lot of money on tracking inconsequential transactions. Thus, it seems likely that *fees are in your future.*

DEVELOP YOUR OWN BEST CUSTOMER IDEAS CHECKLIST

Many companies keep an up-to-date ideas checklist of ways to favor their Best Customers. To help readers wishing to start such a list, the checklist below is offered. It was developed for food retailers, but most of the ideas are transferable to other sectors.

BEST CUSTOMER IDEAS CHECKLIST

Section A: Primarily Price

Make offers to all customers but which favor Best Customers

* Continuity Pricing: eg, for every 12 packets of XYZ cereal one buys in the next six months, receive a $5 gift certificate

* Continuity Program with balloon-end: eg, offer a set of cookware with varying discounts based on the amount spent in the quarter

* Multibuys: on appropriate items offer Buy 3, get 4th free one month, Buy 4 get 5th for 5¢ the following month, etc

* Filters: offer a series of very low prices on promotional items, with a limit of one with every $20 of other purchases

* For every $400 a customer spends in next three months offer a 10% off gift certificate

* Large order discounts on certain items, eg, 20% off purchases over $100 on wine

In a special quarterly Best Customers package include

* An invitation to select five items (from a list of 30 to 40 items) that are regularly bought by Best Customers and, at quarter's end, give them a gift certificate equal to 10% of such purchases

* Certificates for 5% off purchases on the fifth of the first month, 7% on the seventh of the second month and 9% off purchases on ninth of the third month

---

* An offer to buy $500 worth of gift certificates for $450
* A booklet of special offers

Segmented targeted offers to Best Customers only

* Section Zero: target customers with offers in key categories in which they currently aren't shopping (eg, fruit, paper products)
* Opt-in programs: let customer opt into various special program offers
* Break Best Customers into those yielding high, medium, and low gross profit percentages and make different offers appropriate to their profitability and promotional responsiveness

Sales-building programs

* Analyze the results of current subclubs (eg, Baby Club) and see which, if any, increases the number of Best Customers. Introduce other subclubs that are most likely to help build Best Customers.
* On a long-term basis, offer an opportunity to earn air miles based on increases in their total spending.
* Frequency offer: spend $40 in six of the next eight weeks and receive a 10% off certificate.
* Send an offer to try a different signature item over each of the next six weeks. (This builds the long-term sales of these items as well as customer spending.)

Promotions

* Identify those items with high purchase indices among Best Customers for inclusion in your promotional calendar.
* For a limited period, send them scratch-and-win cards, with various hidden percentage-off amounts.

Special pricing privileges for Best Customers

* Private Sale: twice a year advise Best Customers that red-dot items around the store have 10% lower prices for them only. All they have to do is present their card to trigger the lower price. (Preload their card numbers into the point-of-sale system.)

* Offer high-margin items sold by competing channels at very special prices, eg, Dom Pérignon, jewelry, cameras, film, and crystal

* Automatically receive 40% off any film processing in store

Section B: Primarily Recognition
Recognition

* For customers who have spent over $x for the past three (or five) years, send them a gold card which states that they are a Valued Customer since (year).

* Send Best Customers a special sticker to attach to their card entitling them to, say, free coffee at any time in the next six months.

* Reward them with items that have "bragging rights" (eg, free Thanksgiving turkey, ornaments for the Christmas tree, Christmas tree or wreath).

* If you have a points program, offer double points on purchases on their birthday.

* Give customers who spent, say, at least $2,500 last year a *10% off on the 10th of the month certificate,* good for any ten months this year.

* Send special offer certificates with a matching set to give to a friend.

* Send a floral gift on Mother's Day or Thanksgiving.

Privileges

* Invite Best Customers to a special evening at non-competing companies such as a garden center, furniture, or glassware store. Offer special discounts to them.

* Arrange with local theaters to invite Best Customers to a special private preview of a new movie.

Very top Best Customer privileges and rewards

* Treats: send a gift box of very high-quality, self-indulgent cookies once or twice a year.

* Shares: offer opportunity to buy shares in company at the same discount rate as employees

* Free shopping service: invite Best Customers to fax or e-mail their shopping orders for employees to pick and pack

Section C: Primarily Communication

General communications

* Advise Best Customers of any items that they currently buy that are on the up-coming deletion list and suggest alternative items.

* Invite Best Customers to tell us which items they cannot buy in our stores (ie, have to buy elsewhere).

* Have an ongoing thank-you note and/or telephone call program from store management to Best Customers.

* Invite Best Customers to vote for their favorite store associate.

Send postcards to Best Customers advising of

* New season's fruit arriving next week

* Special upcoming new item introductions

* Store management changes

Invite Best Customers to

* Participate in a customer feedback roundtable discussion with the store manager
* A wine tasting with top management to help choose the wine range for the coming year

Quarterly, offer to e-mail to Best Customers

* Three recipes per week, eg, one formal, one quick, and one casual
* Special offers and/or the weekly ad specials
* A mystery coupon offer, from time to time
* Special reminder messages on selected dates

Section D: Other Possibilities

Other Best Customer building ideas

* Have a store contest to see which store can increase their number of Best Customers the most (expressed as a percentage) from one 8-12 week period to another. Objective: To build Best Customer awareness among employees.
* Set up a Best Customer Retention Team in each store. Objective: Develop ways to improve the retention rate of Best Customers.
* Store managers to include in their annual sales budget a target for their top 100 customers and then report on their progress throughout the year.

FIGURE 26: BEST CUSTOMER IDEAS CHECKLIST

TARGETING THE PRIMARY CUSTOMER

Chapter **9**

Loyalty schemes buy you knowledge, not loyalty: loyalty can't be bought.
... Staffan Elinder, Scandinavian direct mailer

W"hat is loyalty? Bits of plastic with points don't make a customer loyal! Loyalty programs are the means, not an end," says Crawford Davidson, head of *Advantage Card* Marketing at Boots The Chemists, UK's leading health and beauty retailer.

Even though 95% of the UK population visits one of Boots' 1,400 stores at least once a year, spending around £4 billion (US$5-6 billion); even though Boots has 26 million customers a month; and even though Boots provides 27% of all health and beauty care in the UK, when it developed its *Advantage Card* program it was designed to appeal most to those it considered its primary customers—women aged 20-45 who were higher spenders on health and beauty and who liked to "treat" themselves.

Boots believes that really looking after this specific customer segment will help translate its vision of being "The world's leading retailer of products and services which help our customers look and feel good about and within themselves" into reality.

Even though this centenarian company (it was founded in 1887 by Jesse Boot) has earned the moniker "Chemists to the Nation", Boots sees itself as a health and beauty retailer, not a drug chain—the term *health and beauty* denoting the concept of well-being, which goes well beyond just filling prescriptions.

Besides its core departments of pharmacy, over-the-counter medicines, and vitamins, a Boots store is known for its excellence in such categories as skin, hair, sun care, toiletries, and cosmetics.

How does one design a loyalty program that has strong appeal to one's primary customer? Through careful analysis and testing. Crawford Davidson, a nuclear physicist by training, is a very insightful marketer. He and his marketing team began by assessing the attributes of the major loyalty programs already operating in the UK and identified the relative position they wanted Boots to have. Figure 27 shows their assessment and their positioning of the Boots program.

They discovered that the majority of the loyalty card programs in place at that time had a male/rational bias with a discount card flavor. The typical supermarket program, although aimed at women, played more to a customer's rational or economic side than to her emotional side. Department stores C&A and BhS were, in Boots' assessment, closer to its own goal of a self-treat, self-indulgence card, with their incorporation of softer rewards such as special evenings and special store privileges in their packages.

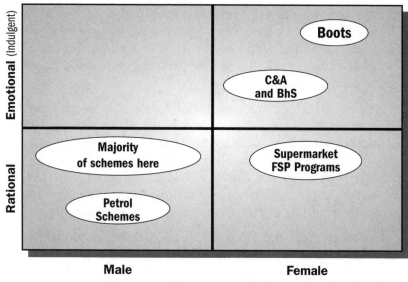

Source: Crawford Davidson

FIGURE 27: BOOTS' COMPETITIVE MATRIX

Positioning yourself is one step. But how does a company that caters to walk-in traffic, with a consequently low transaction size, provide appropriate inducement for its targeted customer to sign up for a loyalty card and readily present it on each visit, without breaking the bank?

Davidson and his team developed an ingenious program. After testing different reward formulas in two distinctly different parts of England (twenty stores in 1995 and nine stores in 1996), Boots rolled out its *Advantage Card* nationwide in late 1997.

THE *ADVANTAGE CARD* PROPOSITION

What was its customer proposition? Instead of the typical UK reward of one point per £1 spent, already popularized by the nation's largest food retailers, Tesco and Sainsbury, Boots offered four points per £1 spent (actually, one point per £0.25) in most categories of products it carried. This was an extremely attractive offer that allowed a meaningful points build-up, given much lower spending in this sector than in the food sector. In addition to points on a customer's total transaction, points could be earned when purchasing certain identified products and when responding to various targeted promotional offers.

At Tesco and Sainsbury, each point earned is worth a penny and can be redeemed against any store purchase, regardless of the transaction's profit margin. Their programs are, effectively, 1% rebate programs. At Boots, each point is also worth a penny, suggesting that *Advantage Card* holders receive a 4% rebate on their card-based spending. At face value, such a program would be extremely expensive for any retailer.

However, the brilliant way in which Boots reconciled the need to appear generous, minimize costs, and reward its primary customer is instructive. *Advantage Card* holders may redeem any of their accumulated points in any transaction but only on items identified with an asterisk next to the price. For example, an asterisked item with a shelf price of £4.50 can be obtained free for 450 points. For its asterisked items, Boots has cleverly selected very high margin, "self-treat" items such as fragrances, oils, and perfumes. This makes the customer feel that she is pampering herself while at the same time offsetting the high cost to Boots of issuing four points for every £1 spent.

Boots has skillfully supported this position with on-going television commercials showing a woman luxuriating in a bathtub, indulging herself, reinforcing the card's unique selling proposition: *A treat for me; not a supplement to my housekeeping budget.* The commercials also reinforce Boots' positive marketplace image.

Another very clever aspect of Boots' reward structure is that the redemption of points has a minimal cannibalization effect on sales because of the indulgent, rather than basic, nature, of the eligible products. At Tesco, for example, where a quarterly points voucher is used by customers as a "cash equivalent", it is thought that at least 75% of the points redeemed simply reduce cash sales. Boots has calculated that less than 25% of points redeemed are used to pay for purchases customers would have made anyway.

How has Boots' differentiated proposition fared? Let the results provide the answer. According to Davidson, in the first year in which the *Advantage Card* went company-wide, Boots achieved a 4% sales gain attributable to the card. Its investment of £25 million was recouped from that gain. Davidson says that in the years since the launch, Boots has sustained the gain.

Internal estimates by Boots indicate that cardholders increased their spending by 10%. Like many successful loyalty card program, transaction counts fell a little and sales rose. Boots' aim was to enroll eight million cardholders within 18 months of launch. In a nation of some 55 million people, the company achieved this goal in half that time. Today, it boasts 12 million cardholders, 93% of whom are women. Of those to whom cards were issued, 9.5 million are currently active, making the *Advantage Card* the UK's largest retail loyalty program.

The *Advantage Card* is now considered by many to be the UK's leading card scheme. From internal research, Boots found that 83% of its cardholders rate it excellent or good. Among all UK women who have a loyalty card, it is the first choice for 50%, and second choice for 35% of them.

From other in-depth research, Boots found that the card was, indeed, seen as more indulgent, more different, more generous, and offering a better reward—right in line with its desired goals.

In addition to the program's sales and profit lift, Boots identifies three other primary benefits from its *Advantage Card* program:

- Insights into customer behavior
- Ability to make targeted offers
- Loyalty

THE POWER OF CUSTOMER INFORMATION

From the outset, it's important to understand that Boots is a highly analytical company. It has kept stock keeping unit (SKU) activity data since the card's inception. Its *Advantage Card* application form has an optional section for customer data beyond the applicant's name and address, such as her age and her children's ages. Boots also enriches its internal data by appending external household data, such as income and ethnicity, purchased from national data companies.

The company's 24-strong analytical team devotes itself to delving into the data, both for systematic and ad hoc analyses, with the overriding goal of providing practical information to help the business operators.

Ian Symis, technical manager of this talented analytical team, gave examples in a presentation to marketers on how Boots uses its customer data.

1. **Product buyer profile.** Using the enriched customer data, Boots has identified the buyer profile (sex, age, income, etc) of key items. This is of immense value as Boots makes targeted offers to its customers from its very diverse range of products.

2. **Promotion analysis.** Boots analyzes all major items promoted each month to see who is buying them. From these analyses, the company has developed its own set of cardholder descriptors such as Deal Seekers, Existing Buyers, Stock-Pilers, and New Customers. This information is used in planning subsequent promotions.

3. **Promotion effectiveness.** Close attention is paid to the breadth and depth of the company's promotions. Is each promoted item sold heavily to just a few customers or is it sold singly to many? What is the promotion's appeal rate among Boots' highest and lowest spenders? Did it attract new customers?

What elements should Boots change if it promotes this item again?

4. **Cross-purchasing analysis.** Using a series of over-lapping colored circles, it examines what other significant items the purchaser of, say, a particular shampoo, buys. The circles may indicate Products X, Y, and Z while, alongside, they show the demographic profiles of these different clusters of customers. This information is helpful in choosing items for future promotions.

5. **Basket analysis.** Boots undertakes a lot of basket analysis (ie, identifying what else is bought in the same transaction) to plan both its shelf layouts and promotions. Bar charts are used to graphically demonstrate the relationships.

6. **Shelf layout.** Using the above Basket analysis and other customer buying behavior analytical tools, Boots has, for example, placed together such departments as Cosmetics and Fragrances, and Skin and Hair Care. Boots then delves further into its analyses and assesses whether these categories should be next to, above or below one other on the shelves. This type of analysis is also done for items within each category.

7. **Customer purchase patterns.** Boots has found that not only are individual customers different from one another, but that the same customer behaves differently in different types of stores at different times of the week. Many have different "at work" and "weekend" stores, and also behave differently when buying different categories. This information has been used in deciding the location of certain promotional items in various stores and, once again, in rearranging the adjacencies of various categories.

8. **Customer loyalty.** One fascinating insight that has come from Boots' analysis is that most customers have a significant loyalty to just one of Boots' diverse health and beauty categories rather than to the whole

repertoire (as is common in food retailing). They have "fragrance" customers, or "skin" customers, or "hair" customers. This knowledge, of course, is very helpful when planning programs to build frequency and sales. It also permits Boots to study changes in customer behavior at the category level rather than at the store level when products are added, deleted, or changed.

9. **New product launch appeal.** Each week after the launch of a new product, the customers buying it for the first time are compared to the repeat buyers. The team graphically shows this with colored block graphs: red for new, green for repeat. If the repeat block is not growing materially over time, they know there is a problem with the new product.

10. **New product launch cannibalization.** After launch, the cannibalization effect of a new product on its two primary competing items (Product A and Product B) is quantified along with the size of the net sales lift of the product category.

"GETTING TO KNOW YOU"

Boots has discovered that the typical *Advantage Card* holder shops in four different stores during the course of a year, exhibiting different behavior characteristics in each. As a result of this finding, as well as having a good appreciation of its customers' demographics, Boots has taken segmentation to a much higher level of sophistication than most retailers. It's somewhat akin to what we saw at Tesco.

For example, a customer may be classified as: Age 25-33; high frequency; and having two shopping modes, Selfless (eg, buying for her baby) and Self-Indulgent (eg, buying fragrances for herself). Common customer descriptors include Brand Loyal, Category Loyal, and Category Shopper. These help paint a picture of the different customer segments Boots serves, and provide the basis for highly selective targeting, especially through Boots' store kiosks.

In addition to a customer's shopping mode (eg, self-indulgent), Boots includes in its customer profiling the customer's life stage (eg, customer's age, age of her children and, therefore, her likely needs), repertoire (ie, which categories the customer buys) and customer economic value. These four elements: Value, Lifestage, Repertoire, and Shopping Mode are the four key building blocks upon which Boots' customer segmentation stands.

Boots also uses its customer profiles in helping decide which items should be promoted throughout the whole chain, which should be included in its targeted mail offers, and which should be included in its even more targeted kiosk offers.

The *Advantage Card,* because it includes a chip (ie, it's a "smart card") is different from most other retailers' cards in that it can record all customer purchases, as well as any identifying characteristics of the customer that the company should choose to download.

POINTS OVER PRICES

Some retailers choose prices as the primary inducement to belong to their loyalty programs. Others choose points. Crawford Davidson recently explained why Boots prefers points:

* Points have greater flexibility.

* Boots has found that on many products, points have led to a greater promotional response than price cuts.

* It is easier to build in an accelerating earning rate for higher spenders using points than using prices.

* Points are a great vehicle for encouraging customers to try new items. For example, Boots has learned that customers are less averse to using points on "risk" items, such as a new range of cosmetics, than offering the same items at a lower price.

* Double-point days, weekends, and special

evenings are a cheaper, more effective way to build sales than cutting prices while, at the same time, they reward the better customers.

❖ Points are "softer" than prices and Boots' target customers respond better to points' promotions than to money-off promotions. For example, Boots has found that an item at £8.50 plus 850 points achieves a better result than a Buy One Get One Free of the same item. Women customers also respond better to, say, a free box of chocolates with a £25 order than a £2 discount off a £25 order (even though the chocolates cost the retailer less). Conversely, points don't work as well on items with a strong price promotional history.

THE BOOTS KIOSK PROGRAM

The company's larger stores have one or more kiosks, enabling it to make individualized offers to customers. After inserting her *Advantage Card* in the kiosk's card reader, the customer's name and points balance appears on the opening screen. Subsequent screens present offers based upon the customer's purchase history and are often refined to anticipate what shopping mode the customer is likely to be in at that particular store. Many of the offers, like those we saw at Superquinn and Harris Teeter, are designed to encourage greater frequency and/or spending.

The offers made via an in-store kiosk—and the responses to them—could also be recorded on the *Advantage Card* itself (as it is a smart card). Despite costing more than loyalty cards with the more common magnetic-stripe or bar-code identifying devices, Boots sees smart cards as one of several pathways leading it closer to its long-term dream of true personalized marketing. This will be possible with a smart card as the customer, in effect, carries her history around with her (including, for example, what offers have been made and accepted in the past). This history is immediately accessible every time the customer uses the card.

In a recent discussion on customer communications, Crawford Davidson succinctly summed up the problems of direct mail today:

❖ It is expensive.

❖ It isn't very flexible.

❖ Items delivered through the post can have a "junk mail" image.

❖ It's often too far removed from the time of sale so that the message can be forgotten.

In contrast, he sees many benefits associated with Boots' kiosk program. In particular, as the customer is in the store at the time of the offer, there is a real-time influence on her decision-making process. It also is relatively low cost, has great flexibility, and it's a form of permission marketing. In addition, he explained, kiosks can:

❖ Build value for loyal customers

❖ Build loyalty among customers

❖ Build brands and categories by providing both information and offers

❖ Solicit trial from passers-by

❖ Incentivize cross-shopping across categories

❖ Drive spending, shopping breadth, and frequency

❖ Direct value to the most value conscious customer

❖ Provide a low-cost vehicle to conduct customer research and surveys

❖ Run quizzes (eg, How often should you change your toothbrush?) and then use the customer's answers on subsequent trips to offer her appropriate promotions (eg, a toothbrush)

❖ Prequalify planned mailings to reduce costs by asking customers various questions (eg, Would you like to receive information on ... travel, health insurance, banking, credit cards, oral hygiene, etc?)

THE BOTTOM LINE

As this overview suggests, Boots is using its customer information as a strategic tool, quietly adding to its successes of the past century.[1]

---

[1] The reader should be aware that just before this book went to press, Davidson announced that he was leaving Boots to become head of the Tesco Clubcard program. It will be interesting to follow the evolution of both programs over the next few years.

A RETAILER'S VIEW

To gain another insight into this global leader, let's see how Crawford Davidson answered my two basic loyalty questions.

Crawford, what's your bottom line on the Advantage Card?

"Our loyalty card is an added-value proposition in a retailer with an added-value strategy. We believe we have gained about 3% of sales annually because of its existence and a further 5% has been created though activity driven by the loyalty program. The role of the loyalty card is to identify our best customers and to allow us to tailor our offer to meet their needs."

Why, then, don't all retailers have a loyalty card program?

"If everyone had a loyalty program then the question would be: whose program is most clearly differentiated? Retailers with a value proposition tend to find that the costs of running a loyalty program are best directed through offers. After all, if you don't intend to tailor your offer by customer groups, why would you even need to identify customers?"

PART III

HOW CUTOMER MEASUREMENTS HELP

CHAPTER 10: INFINITE SEGMENTATION

Information benefits for the marketing department

One immediate benefit of gathering customer data is that we learn how diverse our customers are: each group (segment) represents different interests, economics, and opportunities.

CHAPTER 11: THE GREAT GAME OF YIELD

Information benefits for the whole company

This is the pot of gold at the end of the information rainbow: customer information diffused throughout the organization helping to improve performance in all areas. A number of successes are described; some still await discovery.

INFINITE SEGMENTATION

Chapter **10**

How do I segment thee? Let me count the ways.
... with apologies to Elizabeth Barrett Browning

Round up the usual suspects.
        ... Captain Louis Renault (Claude Rains)
                in the movie *Casablanca*

Customers are different. They spend different amounts. They buy different items. They have different ages, incomes, and family sizes. They drive different distances to our stores. They have different lifestyles and attitudes. Some are price conscious; others are not. Some have just begun shopping with us; others have been with us for years. Some spend most of their money with us; others a small fraction. Some shop daily; others quarterly. Some shop most departments; others just a few. Not only are customers different, they can, and do, exhibit different characteristics in different stores on different shopping occasions.

Welcome to the world of customer segmentation!

Segmentation is sorting customers with common characteristics into separate groups. The definition is simple; the practice is complex, for the number of ways to segment appears to be infinite.

Why do marketers get so excited about segmentation? Because it builds better profits. By identifying customers with better sales and profit characteristics, we can market more heavily to them and their clones and reduce our spending on those without such characteristics. By making appropriate offers at the right time to customers with specific needs, we make everybody happy: the customer who receives the relevant, timely offer; the other customers for not receiving irrelevant offers ("junk mail"); and our shareholders for increasing sales at least cost.

Our challenge is that segmentation is an imperfect science. No database, in reality, can store all the information we would like to have about our customers, and no customer would give us all the information we desire to know about her, and keep it current for us. Therefore, to win in this arena, we simply have to be more effective at segmentation than our competitors.

In the earlier chapters of this book, we saw examples of segmentation. In particular, Tesco's impressive approach was outlined. This chapter will continue the discussion and cover some of the many other ways retailers segment their customers, along with some of the lessons learned. But first, some background.

RECENCY, FREQUENCY, SPENDING

Catalog and other direct mail pioneers added two highly valuable segmentation tools to our measurement arsenal. The first was decile reporting. The second was RFM (Recency, Frequency, Monetary) analysis. The former was discussed in Chapter 3 and the latter will be covered here.

The idea of targeting offers to customers based upon their recency, frequency, and monetary value is the bedrock of direct marketers. Then some smart retailers discovered that segmentation wasn't something just for catalog companies; it also could help them cost-effectively build sales. However, they made one small change to RFM: they called it RFS (Recency, Frequency, Spending), because spending (or sales) is a more natural part of their vernacular than "monetary".

What the early direct marketers found (as did the retail converts) was that there are three rules which, when followed, give the best responses to any direct marketing campaign:

* The more *recently* a customer has shopped, the better she responds and spends.

* The more *frequently* a customer has shopped, the better she responds and spends.

* The more a customer has *spent* with us, the better she responds and spends.

Given these findings, it was logical for marketers to sort their databases from best to worst as a preliminary step in segmenting their customers:

* From most recent to least recent

* From most frequent to least frequent

* From highest spender to lowest spender

The direct marketers, with their affinity for deciles, split each of the above segments into five groups of two deciles each (called quintiles) and gave each quintile a descriptor code. For example, those customers who were among the most recent purchasers (the top 20%) were designated as R1 and those who were among the least recent purchasers (the bottom 20%) were coded as R5. In like manner, customers were coded with F1 ... F5 to describe their frequency ranking and S1 ... S5 to describe their spending ranking.

Direct marketers went further and sorted customers based upon various combinations of their recency, frequency, and spending. This followed the realization that a customer with an R1 F1 S1 classification was usually a far more attractive target than one with, say, an R3 F3 S3 or an R5 F5 S5 classification.

Not only did such customers have the perfect profile—what more could you want than someone who was most recently a buyer from you, was a frequent buyer and was also one of your highest spending customers?—but these were also the customers who responded best to your promotional offers. Conversely, the lowest payback came from those with R5 F5 S5 characteristics.

Mathematically inclined readers will quickly calculate that direct marketers using this RFS-quintile approach had 125 customer segments ($5 \times 5 \times 5 = 125$). Such a large number of segments made sense for many of the catalog companies with large customer files and who often used three or more years of transaction history. However, retailers in sectors where customers shop frequently found that such a large set of segments was of little practical value to them.

Food retailers, for example, have found that if a customer has not shopped in the past quarter (12 or 13 weeks) or, even more generously, two quarters (24 or 26 weeks), the chances of her returning as a regular, average spending customer are slim to none. So they devised a much simpler matrix. They sorted customers into just two groups based on their recency, frequency, and spending rankings, such as the top 30% and bottom 70% in each of recency, frequency, and spending. This meant that food retailers ended up with a very sleek and manageable 8-segment ($2 \times 2 \times 2 = 8$) customer breakout.

However, for readers new to this important concept, let's walk through the simple step-by-step RFS methodology before looking at two detailed 8-segment RFS examples.

A SIMPLE EXAMPLE OF RFS

Let's imagine a company with just 10 customers that has prepared a summary of its customer activity for a recent 24-week period (Table 28). It shows:

- ❖ Column (a): Customers sorted in sequence.

- ❖ Column (b): The date each customer last shopped.

- ❖ Columns (c-d): How many times each shopped ("visited") and spent in the review period. For example, during the 24-week review period, the Beck household shopped 78 times spending a total of $295.20.

- ❖ Column (e): Each customer's *Recency,* ie, the number of days from her last visit to the last day of the review period. For example, as the Beck household's last shopping visit was June 17th, the same day as the last day of the review period, their recency is zero days.

- ❖ Columns (f-h): Each customer's average number of visits per week during the review period (regardless of when she last shopped), the average amount spent per visit, and the average amount spent per week. For example, the Beck Household's average number of Visits Per Week (VPW) was 3.25 (78 ÷ 24 = 3.25), their average Spend Per Visit (SPV) was $3.78 ($295.20 ÷ 78 = $3.78), and their average Spending Per Week (SPW) was $12.30 ($295.20 ÷ 24 = $12.30). Their average Spend Per Visit can also be calculated by dividing their Spend Per Week by the average number of Visits Per Week ($12.30 ÷ 3.25 = $3.78).

It is upon such simple data that the mighty RFS edifice is built.

Review Period: Sunday, January 2 - Saturday, June 17

(i)	**Weeks in Review Period**	24
(j)	**Review Period Last Date**	17 – Jun

ID #	Customer Name	Date Last Shopped in 24 weeks	Tot.Shopping Visits in 24 weeks	Total Spending ($) in 24 weeks	Recency (# Days)	VPW #	SPV $	SPW $
(a)		(b)	(c)	(d)	(e) = j – b	(f) = c/i	(g) = d/c	(h) = d/i
101	Beck	17 – Jun	78	295.20	0	3.25	3.78	12.30
102	Dale	2 – Jun	38	1,211.52	15	1.58	31.88	50.48
103	Hall	30 – May	60	1,256.16	18	2.50	20.94	52.34
104	Kent	16 – Jun	15	1,488.24	1	0.63	99.22	62.01
105	Oak	15 – Jun	19	674.64	2	0.79	35.51	28.11
106	Park	2 – Feb	2	289.92	136	0.08	144.96	12.08
107	Rice	29 – Mar	15	549.84	80	0.63	36.66	22.91
108	Snow	18 – May	58	1,090.56	30	2.42	18.80	45.44
109	Teal	14 – Jun	47	1,501.92	3	1.96	31.96	62.58
110	Wade	11 – Apr	26	240.00	67	1.08	9.23	10.00

TABLE 28: RFS TEN CUSTOMER BASE

(a)	(b)	(c)
Sorted by Recency		
1	101	Beck
2	104	Kent
3	105	Oak
4	109	Teal
5	102	Dale
6	103	Hall
7	108	Snow
8	110	Wade
9	107	Rice
10	106	Park

(d)	(e)	(f)
Sorted by Frequency		
1	101	Beck
2	103	Hall
3	108	Snow
4	109	Teal
5	102	Dale
6	110	Wade
7	105	Oak
8	104	Kent
9	107	Rice
10	106	Park

(g)	(h)	(i)
Sorted by Spending		
1	109	Teal
2	104	Kent
3	103	Hall
4	102	Dale
5	108	Snow
6	105	Oak
7	107	Rice
8	101	Beck
9	106	Park
10	110	Wade

(j)	(k)	(l)		
ID	Customer	Segment		
101	Beck	R1	F1	S2
102	Dale	R2	F2	S2
103	Hall	R2	F1	S1
104	Kent	R1	F2	S1
105	Oak	R1	F2	S2
106	Park	R2	F2	S2
107	Rice	R2	F2	S2
108	Snow	R2	F2	S2
109	Teal	R2	F2	S1
110	Wade	R2	F2	S2

TABLE 29: RFS TEN CUSTOMER SORTS

The basic steps of RFS classification are shown in Table 29. Using the information in Table 28, customers are ranked from best to worst for their recency, frequency, and spending. For example, the Beck household has the best recency (0 days), while the Park household has the worst (it was 136 days before June 17th when they last shopped). Frequency and total spending are sorted in a similar manner.

The example in Table 29 uses a 30/70 break (ie, the top 30% of each group is coded R1 or F1 or S1 and the bottom 70% is R2 or F2 or S2), as seen in the first three subtables of Table 29 (col. a-i). Once sorted like this, each household can have its segmentation code for each review period appended in the database as shown in the right hand subtable (col. j-l). We see in this subtable, for example, that the Beck household is coded R1 F1 S2 whereas the Dale household is coded as R2 F2 S2.

As mentioned, there are only eight combinations in a two-split RFS table, as seen in Figure 30, below.

1	R1	F1	S1
2	R1	F1	S2
3	R1	F2	S1
4	R1	F2	S2
5	R2	F1	S1
6	R2	F1	S2
7	R2	F2	S1
8	R2	F2	S2

FIGURE 30: TWO-SPLIT RFS

What the direct marketers found long ago, and retailers more recently, is that each cell has a different response rate to promotional offers. Thus, by understanding what they are, along with the accompanying changes in each cell's total spending (less the mailing and markdown costs), we are able to rank them from the most profitable to least profitable. Thereafter, we can use that knowledge each time we have a targeted promotion.

Of course, not every offer will yield the same response, not every cell always responds in the same way to each promotion and, if we communicate too much to the same customers, they suffer what direct marketers call "list fatigue"—their response rates decline from being overused. That's where the experience of the marketer comes in. It's where a company steeped in segmentation gains an edge over its less experienced competitors.

RFS IN PRACTICE

My first experience with RFS was a challenge from a retailer that had a market share of over 15% of its country's food business. The company was mailing its promotional circular to the top 60% of its shoppers and wanted to reduce this cost. The solution was an RFS table like we see in Table 31. We did a 60/40 split and then selected those in cell 1 (R1 F1 S1) to receive the circulars.

Note that even though we identified the top 60% of customers in each of our recency, frequency and spending sorts, only 44.1% (row 1, col. i) were in this prime grouping. Just because you may be among the most recent of shoppers, it doesn't follow that you, automatically, are also among the most frequent and/or highest spenders.

Instead of mailing to the top 60% as in the past, the company then mailed those customers in the prime R1 F1 S1 cell (ie, 44.1% of the base) as well as to any new customers in the last three months, regardless of their spending levels. The company cut circular distribution by over 20% with no adverse effect on sales.

RFS8 [60/40]

Review Period: Weeks 1-24

Olympic Scale: Top 60% = 1. Bottom 40% = 2

(m) 24 Weeks

(e)=c/a/m (f) = h/c

	Cell Description	(a) #Cust. in Cell	(b) # New Cust.	(c) # of Visits (ie, Trans.)	(d) Recency # Days	(e)=c/a/m Freq. VisitsPW	(f)=h/c Spending Per Visit	(g) Spending Per Week	(h) 24 Week Total ($K)	(i) = (a) % of Cust.	(j) = (b) %New Cust.	(k) = (c) % of Trans.	(l) = (h) % of Spending
1	R1 F1 S1	4,406	264	125,108	4.4	1.18	$24.92	$29.49	3,118	44.1	16.1	77.4	77.1
2	R1 F1 S2	496	85	7,237	5.1	0.61	8.57	5.21	62	5.0	5.2	4.5	1.5
3	R1 F2 S1	312	69	1,764	6.1	0.24	55.56	13.09	98	3.1	4.2	1.1	2.4
4	R1 F2 S2	786	327	2,771	5.9	0.15	22.02	3.23	61	7.8	19.9	1.7	1.5
5	R2 F1 S1	828	51	13,900	30.1	0.70	28.56	19.98	397	8.3	3.1	8.6	9.8
6	R2 F1 S2	270	29	3,224	36.7	0.50	9.93	4.94	32	2.7	1.8	2.0	0.8
7	R2 F2 S1	454	61	2,280	41.3	0.21	60.09	12.57	137	4.5	3.7	1.4	3.4
8	R2 F2 S2	2,448	756	5,252	69.9	0.09	26.66	2.38	140	24.5	46.0	3.3	3.5
	Totals	10,000	1,642	161,536	25.3	0.67	$25.04	$16.85	4,045	100.0	100.0	100.0	100.0

Results expressed per 10,000 Households

TABLE 31: RETAILER RFS (60/40) MATRIX

RFS8 [30/70]

Olympic Scale: Top 30% = 1. Bottom 70% = 2 (m) | 24 | Weeks

Review Period: Weeks 1-24

		(a)	(b)	(c)	(d)	(e)=c/a/m	(f) = h/c	(g)	(h)	(i) = (a)	(j) = (b)	(k) = (c)	(l) = (h)
	Cell Description	#Cust. in Cell	# New Cust.	# of Visits (ie, Trans.)	Recency # Days	Freq. Visits PW	Spending ($) Per Visit	Spending ($) Per Week	24 Week Total ($K)	% of Cust.	%New Cust.	% of Trans.	% of Spending
1	R1 F1 S1	1,240	39	56,002	2.0	1.88	$23.00	$43.24	1,288	12.4	2.4	34.7	31.8
2	R1 F1 S2	524	42	17,103	2.1	1.36	10.11	13.76	173	5.2	2.5	10.6	4.3
3	R1 F2 S1	258	19	3,820	2.2	0.63	51.05	32.16	195	2.6	1.2	2.4	4.8
4	R1 F2 S2	978	248	9,154	2.1	0.39	22.07	8.61	202	9.8	15.1	5.7	5.0
5	R2 F1 S1	797	19	24,484	9.5	1.28	31.65	40.52	775	8.0	1.2	15.2	19.2
6	R2 F1 S2	439	24	12,011	13.7	1.14	11.66	13.29	140	4.4	1.4	7.4	3.5
7	R2 F2 S1	706	40	9,828	13.9	0.58	54.95	31.87	540	7.1	2.4	6.1	13.3
8	R2 F2 S2	5,058	1,211	29,134	44.2	0.24	25.13	6.03	732	50.6	73.8	18.0	18.1
	Totals	10,000	1,642	161,536	25.3	0.67	$25.04	$16.85	4,045	100.0	100.0	100.0	100.0

Note: Roundings affect some of the above calculations

Results expressed per 10,000 Households

TABLE 32: RETAILER RFS (30/70) MATRIX

More commonly, however, RFS segmentation is used for targeting customers with product offers or spending incentives. In these cases, the split may be flipped so that a smaller but higher quality group is included in the R1 F1 S1 category. To show the effect of such a flip, Table 32 is a 30/70 split of the same data used in Table 31 (60/40 split), as reflected in the identical bottom rows of both tables.

Looking at the individual cells 1 through 8 in both tables, we see the effect of these two significantly different combinations. The 60/40 split puts 44.1% of the customers in the top cell (row 1), generating 77.1% of the sales, whereas the 30/70 split puts only 12.4% of the customers in the top cell, generating 31.8% of the sales. The bottom cell (cell 8) is, as expected, a mirror image of the top: the 60/40 split places 24.5% of the customers there, providing only 3.5% of sales, whereas the 30/70 split places 50.6% of the customers there, providing 18.1% of the sales.

DEFINE YOUR BUSINESS OBJECTIVE FIRST

Asking the question, *What is our business objective?* is the starting point with all segmentation exercises. Segmentation must be driven by business goals, and the results from the segmented marketing efforts should be seen as supporting specific goals and measured accordingly.

The right split will depend upon the objective together with the nature and cost of what's being offered. Likewise, we need to select the right components. Should we, for example, consider factors other than RFS—eg, distance from store, ethnicity, or degree of customer price elasticity?

Over the years, I have seen companies:

❖ Exclude new customers from their RFS matrix because such customers aren't comparable to the others, as they shop, on average, only half of the review period.

❖ Use three splits (eg, 30/40/30) but only two factors (frequency and spending) over a three-month base (ie, they assumed that everyone who shopped within three months is recent). Incidentally, this mix gives nine cells (3 x 3).

❖ Use fixed thresholds over time for their recency, frequency, and spending (eg, visited over 1.0 times per week and spent over $50 per week) and then measure improvements in the "better" cells. (This approach supports a Best Customer strategy.)

❖ Use a six-month base of data but put all customers who didn't shop in the last three months in a new ninth row, labeled *Inactives*. The active customers are then sorted using the split chosen. (This approach gives a richer base of active customers.)

❖ Add an *external* fourth factor besides recency, frequency, and spending. One large shoe chain has improved its targeting effectiveness by adding the distance from a customer's home to the nearest store, classifying the distances as either Near or Far.

❖ Add an *internal* fourth factor such as customers' gross profit percentage or their total spending in a certain category. Department stores often do this when planning a promotion for that category. Remember, the purpose of segmentation is to identify the most likely prospects for the offer.

The possible range of combinations is almost endless. And the more we work with RFS segmentation, testing the effect of different factors and splits, measuring the different cells responses, and understanding the composition of each cell, the more sophisticated marketers we become.

Readers interested in deepening their understanding of how direct marketers segment and measure their responses should go to either of Arthur Hughes' eminently readable books: *The Complete Database Marketer* and *Strategic Database Marketing*. Both books have excellent sections on this subject.

UNDERSTANDING CUSTOMERS BETTER

In my early work with RFS, two cells in particular fascinated me. They were numbers 3 and 7 (R1 F2 S1 and R2 F2 S1). These comprise customers who don't shop very often but when they do, they spend big (ie, they have low F and high S scores). Looking at Table 31, for example, their average Spend Per Visit of $55.56 (row 3,f) and $60.09 (row 7,f) is more than double that of the best cell ($24.92) (row 1,f) and the company average ($25.04) (row 9,f). What would be required to encourage these high spenders to shop more often?

First, we had to learn more about the customers populating these cells—which we could readily do, thanks to the data provided by their loyalty cards. A study of where these customers lived relative to the stores where they shopped, carried out in tandem with phone-based customer research, revealed some interesting customer types.

One type is what I call the "mountain men", those customers who come out of the hills (or off the farms) once a month for a big, fill-the-pantry trip. Another type, a variation of the mountain men that surprised one company researching its RFS cell compositions, were various groups of women who drove 50-100 miles once a month to the regional city where its stores were located to stock up. This company has such an outstanding reputation for quality that women in distant towns forsake their local stores to make a special day's outing to shop them.

Another puzzle were those who populated cell 2 (R1 F1 S2). Who were these customers who shopped with high regularity but didn't spend much in total? At one supermarket chain, we found that this particular cell included a high number of office employees. They regularly frequented its salad bars at lunchtime but, otherwise, did not do their primary shopping at the chain. Another unique marketing challenge!

Such customer insights remind us once again that our customers are definitely not all equal and that only when we understand the composition and behavior of the diverse segments and micro-segments of our customer database can we be intelligent, effective marketers. Over time, as we seek ways to improve our marketing yield—as we wallow in the numbers and nuances of our database—we develop an appreciation for our different customer profiles and the various rules of thumb that come with them.

LESSONS FROM OTHERS

Over the years I have heard many speeches by leading marketing practitioners. Three in particular come to mind as we discuss segmentation.

In a Kansas City presentation, Bob Stone, one of the sages of direct marketing, shared some guidelines with us, drawing on his decades of marketing experience:

- ❖ Mailing lists purchased from other companies containing names of those who have responded to offers in the last six months are usually the most productive.
- ❖ The pull for any list varies during the year and will also vary by region, zip code, and census tract.
- ❖ People over 35 tend to respond at a greater rate than those under 35.
- ❖ Rural areas tend to respond at a greater rate than do urban areas.

Second, Bonnie Predd, who managed the WaldenBook Preferred Reader program, reminded a Direct Marketing Association audience of the segmentation pitfalls of appending cluster codes to customers. Using block-group characteristics was certainly not viable for her book selling business and nor, by implication, for some others.

She had found that neighbors, despite having similarly priced homes and, possibly, similar incomes, had quite dissimilar reading habits. Based on the lessons she had learned from her database, one home owner may buy books only twice a year, each time spending $40 on a couple of Tom

Clancy thrillers. Yet the next-door neighbor may visit a bookstore twice a week and spend $400 in a year. So much for the "birds of a feather flock together" cluster code mindset. For certain businesses, cluster coding just doesn't work: customers are as individual as their toothbrushes.

Third, at the 1998 Seklemian/Newell Conference in Chicago, David Walker gave a fascinating presentation on some of the things he had learned as vice president of marketing at Kids R Us. From 10 million customers in his database, he found six primary types at his stores:

- ❖ Super shoppers (who had high RFS scores)
- ❖ Power shoppers (heavy shoppers, particularly during the back-to-school season)
- ❖ Occasional shoppers (who shopped only once or twice a year)
- ❖ First timers (trying out the company)
- ❖ Holiday shoppers (primarily Christmas shoppers)
- ❖ Baby buyers (who buy only baby items)

Here was a marketer who had studied his customers' characteristics and had come up with a set of rules appropriate to his sector. Based upon these distinct customer types, he marketed to each accordingly. Among the super shoppers, for example, he worked at gaining an even larger share of wallet, with special offers of new or exclusive merchandise along with higher-margin offerings. First-time customers were targeted and managed for rapid return.

Customers who showed cross-shopping potential and others who were transitioning to new categories (eg, families with babies who were becoming "kids") were appropriately targeted. Single-department niche customers were targeted to broaden their shopping experience.

Zip codes and subzip codes that had the highest new customer growth were identified for special mailings.

Quite obviously, here was a company using customer data to support its business goals.

SEGMENTATION POSSIBILITIES ARE ENDLESS

Segmentation possibilities are endless. Others include:

- ❖ Customer share of wallet (how much she spends with us as a share of her total spending)
- ❖ Customer elasticity (how responsive a customer is to our promotions)
- ❖ Behavior characteristics (eg, smokers or those who are diet conscious)
- ❖ Higher-spending groups (eg, those with babies, children, and/or pets in the family)
- ❖ The number of departments or categories in which customers shop in our stores
- ❖ Higher-spending customers who don't buy certain basic items (eg, supermarkets have found that Best Customers who are not buying their paper products are usually buying them at a warehouse club)

As we think of all of our segmentation opportunities, keep in mind that there is one major hurdle we have to jump: we need a low cost delivery vehicle for our offers. The ideal would be e-mail and the Internet, both of which are essentially free. Alas, for most retailers today, only a small percentage of their customers use those media actively for promotional material, so they are forced to communicate in other ways.

For many retailers, mail is the most expensive option unless it is part of a cooperative program where suppliers are paying the mailing costs. In-store, differentiated communication using checkout printers, dispensers, or kiosks are the current preferred lower-cost options. The cost of your offer delivery vehicle will, of course, influence the nature and amount of segmented marketing that you undertake.

THE BOTTOM LINE

Loyalty marketing is all about gathering information so that we can make cost-effective, differentiated offers to our customers. Differentiation is segmentation. As we begin to comprehend the diversity of our customer base, we start to see the opportunities. Not necessarily for big bang gains but for hundreds of small yield gains which, collectively, give a solid boost to profits.

THE GREAT GAME OF YIELD

Chapter **11**

Which one activity is at the center of costs and of results? The answer: serving the customer. Thus it is the yield per customer— both the volume of services a customer uses and the mix of those services—that determines costs and profitability.

... Peter Drucker

Do 1000 things just 1% better and soon you'll be 1000% better.

... Tom Peters

The primary purpose of a business is to profitably acquire, satisfy, and retain customers. The primary purpose of a loyalty card program is to provide information to assist in achieving these objectives. Customer information is used to help acquire and retain customers (ie, build loyalty). It is also used to help accomplish other business goals such as finding the right location for a new store, having the right product assortment, and monitoring the chain's quality, service, and friendliness. Customer information also helps lower costs by helping identify inefficient and wasteful spending, particularly wasteful expenditure on low yield customers. Customer information is a powerful ally.

KNOWLEDGE PRECEDES INTELLIGENT PLANNING

Imagine trying to train to run a four-minute mile without a time monitor: a stopwatch. Imagine trying to run a business without a customer monitor: a report containing key customer measurements.

The First Act of a loyalty program is about profitably establishing an attractive offer, so that a customer believes it is in her best interests to apply for and use the company's new loyalty card. The Second Act is all about using the information collected to intelligently increase the customer yield.

Often, it's not one big factor but a combination of many small elements that underpin continued success. It's doing all the little things right, as Tom Peters says. A successful farmer, be he an American wheat farmer, a Japanese rice farmer, or a New Zealand sheep farmer, increases the yield of his land in many, many ways—not just one.

Increasing the yield from our customer base is no different. We seek small improvements from every part of our database: from our long-standing and new customers; from our heavy- and low-spenders; from our high-and volatile-frequency customers; and from those who shop one department, or all, or just buy what's on promotion.

THE GREAT GAME OF YIELD

This is the great game of yield! Customers are not equal: even customers spending similar amounts with us have different motivations and purchase patterns.

Yield management is managing the many aspects of our customer data to optimize our long-term profit. Yield management is the logic behind a Best Customer program or a Baby Club. Yield management is the *sine qua non* in selecting one store site over others. Yield management is the impetus for eliminating circular distribution in areas sparsely populated by Best Customers. Yield management is the economic calculus behind tying promotional offers to the spending levels of customers. Yield management is the bottom line of all business—the optimizing of returns from the limited resources under our stewardship.

This book already is replete with examples of how loyalty leaders are using customer information to improve their yields. The rest of this chapter will add more hues to the picture already painted.

CIRCULAR EFFICIENCY

Often, one of the first priorities of a company with a new, solid base of customer data is to improve the efficiency with which it distributes circulars. Using customer data, it can now compare the areas where its better customers live with the areas where its circulars are being distributed; then cut back on circular distribution to low-spending customers and areas with low response to previous communications.

The potential impact of such a fact-based action is well illustrated in a speech given several years ago by Steve Burrows, director of retail operations of the Hale-Halsell Company, based in Tulsa, Oklahoma:

> Some time after the card launch in our Super-H stores, we utilized our zip code report to more efficiently reach our customers and were able to cut 25% of our ad copies. We requested a name and address report for five area zip codes where we were sending 20,000 ads—and where we are now sending only 750 ads directly to our card customers in those areas. We will save $250,000 this year in our 14 stores—all previously wasted. This is just the tip of the iceberg. We had been sending out ads weekly, equal to three times our customer count! I am using 50% of this to finish paying off my program expense and the other 50% goes straight to my bottom line. After one year, advertising expense has been cut dramatically.

Other uses of customer data in the advertising area, besides distribution effectiveness, include:

❖ Ad item selection (identifying which items appeal more to both our most and least valuable customers and altering the ad accordingly)

❖ Ad space effectiveness (testing how many ad pages or column inches can be reduced without losing good customers or hurting profits)

❖ Ad frequency effectiveness (testing how often the company needs to run advertisements—weekly? fortnightly? monthly? quarterly?—without losing good customers)

MINIMIZING THE IMPACT OF NEW COMPETITORS

Another area where customer knowledge has yielded material cost savings is in the way in which companies have responded to store openings by competitors. The traditional response has been an expensive across-the-board pre- and post-opening promotional effort: rather like blasting a shotgun into the night in the direction of a fearsome sound.

Once armed with customer information, however, a company can respond selectively to those customers who are most likely to be attracted to the new store. The response can also be more appropriate, with retention offers relative to the value of the individual customer. In addition, the targeted offers are often made stealthily, either by mail or via the in-store checkout printers or kiosks. This neutralizes the possibility of the new competitor knowing either the extent of the communications or being able to outbid the offers, apart from making a costly offer to everyone.

One loyalty leader has developed its competitive response to a fine art. Whenever one of its stores is threatened by a competitor's new store, this leader identifies from its database where its customers live in relation to its threatened store and to the new store. Then, based upon each customer's past spending, her location, and driving times to both stores, the company estimates the potential loss of sales its store will suffer as a result of the new competitive opening.

This is achieved by breaking the market area into geographic segments and, within each, classifying its store's customers into different value segments, ie, identifying the Diamonds, Rubies, Opals, Pearls, and New Customers. For each of these spending/location segments, estimates are made of the likelihood of defection to the competitor.

A decision is then made as to which segments will get priority retention attention and what will be spent on each segment. The higher-spending customers in the "at risk" segments receive the most attention and receive a flow of offers of various free, high-quality signature items from its store. Experiencing the signature items reminds these high-spending customers that there is only one store in the area where they can buy such quality—and it's not the new competitor's store!

Another example, from a regional chain I admire, shows how customer knowledge was used to stop another excellent regional chain from gaining a foothold in its marketplace.

The formidable competitor (which we'll call Red Stores) had received a building permit to build a much larger store on the same parking lot as one of this company's (Blue Stores) smaller, older stores.

In anticipation of the competitive move, Blue Stores extensively remodeled its smaller store. As one would expect, store conditions were bad for customers during the remodeling. Before it began remodeling, sales were more than $300,000 per week. During the remodeling, they dropped by over 40% in some weeks. The store even had to close for a few days. Upon completion of its remodeling, Blue Stores identified in its database the many thousands of customers who were regular shoppers in that store. A letter was sent to them, advising them that the remodeling was over, thanked them for their patience, and enclosed some special offers.

All but 183 customers returned to the store. Unhappy with even this excellent result (that's the inherent nature of great companies!), Blue Stores asked the store management team to send a handwritten note to each of these customers, enclosing a $10 gift certificate and an invitation to come back and see the newly remodeled store. All but three returned.

Then, four weeks before the competitive opening, Blue Stores again mailed the store's entire database, offering a $5-off gift certificate good with a $50 order for each of the next twelve weeks. In addition, any customer using all twelve would be mailed a $10 gift certificate. In questioning the company whether this was overkill, I was told that even though this action cost the company $10,000 a week, it was cheaper than losing—forever—a large number of customers to its outstanding competitor.

Blue Stores was delighted with the results. Its store sales jumped 6-7% in the months following the competitive opening. Further, it learned that the new store of Red Stores, almost twice the size of their's, was doing less than half of the remodeled Blue store's sales, and Red Stores weren't sure why! Without a loyalty card program of its own, Red Stores wasn't even able to selectively target its customers.

THE FALSE CRY FOR NEW CUSTOMERS

Store operations executives are always asking for promotions to attract more new customers in order to boost sales. There are two problems with this obsession. Most new customers attracted by the promotion won't stay with us for long. In addition, the overwhelming majority of those who do stay are among the lowest spenders for a long time.

A claim like this, until recently, would have been vigorously debated, with each side using many anecdotal stories about various customers to buttress its side of the argument. Now, customer data has pricked yet another balloon of hot-aired opinion.

One leading retailer's four-year profile of new customer behavior, shown in Table 33, illustrates what false hope the cry for new customers contains. Instead, the cry should be an anguished one—a cry calling for better ways to retain and up-sell those new customers who come to our stores.

Table 33 is taken from nine months of data. Results are expressed per 1,000 new customers. It shows how many new customers (ie, used the company's loyalty card for the first time in a quarter) came back and shopped in the following quarter (col. b); and returned to shop in the same quarter they signed up in, one, two, three and four years later (cols. c-f). It also shows how many did not shop in the subsequent quarters (row 5).

We see, for example, that in the same calendar quarter one year later (col. c), of every 1,000 new customers only two were Diamonds (spending over $100 per week) and 12 were Rubies (spending $50-$100 per week), or 0.2% and 1.2%, respectively, of the total. In other words, only 1.4% had become Best Customers. And of the New Customers who were active a year later, most—421 of the 465 who returned—spent less than $25 per week (rows 4,5,6, col. c).

Of every 1,000 New Customers, how much they spent in later quarters

			(a)	(b)	(c)	(d)	(e)	(f)
	Base Qtr.		SPW	Q + 1	Q + 4	Q + 8	Q + 12	Q + 16
1		D	>$100	2	2	1	3	2
2	**Later**	R	$50-$100	12	12	13	13	10
3	**Spending**	O	$25-$50	29	30	28	31	32
4	**Levels**	P	< $25	504	421	306	273	279
5			Inactive	453	535	652	680	677
6			Total	1,000	1,000	1,000	1,000	1,000

Results Per 1,000 New Households   *2/1,000 = 0.2%; 453/1,000 =45.3%, etc*

Summary Groups expressed as % of Total New Customers

7	Best Cust.	BC	>$50	1.4%	1.4%	1.4%	1.6%	1.2%
8	Key Cust.	KC	>$25	4.3%	4.4%	4.2%	4.7%	4.4%

Summary Groups expressed as % of Total New Customers

9	Best Cust.	BC	>$50	2.6%	3.0%	4.0%	5.0%	3.7%
10	Key Cust.	KC	>$25	7.9%	9.5%	12.1%	14.7%	13.6%

Results drawn from 9 months of data

How to Read

Col. c: *One year (ie,4 Qtrs) after customers first shopped 0.2% were Diamonds, 1.2% were Rubies, 3.0% were Opals, 42.1% were Pearls, and the majority, 53.5% were inactive.*
Row 9: *Of those active one year after first shopping, 3.0% were BCs.*

TABLE 33: NEW CUSTOMER SPENDING OVER FOUR YEARS

SOME HIGHLIGHTS OF TABLE 33

Where did every 1,000 new customers end up?

- One year later, two were Diamonds and 12 were Rubies. That means that only 14 (1.4%) had become Best Customers.

- In the same time period, 421 (42.1%) were Pearls and 535 (53.5%) were inactive. In other words, a massive 95.6% of the New Customers were in the lowest spending bracket or didn't return to shop.

How consistent were they?

- In all of the five quarters featured, covering four years, the Best Customers (Diamonds and Rubies) were between 1.2% and 1.6% of the total.

- In the same time period, the percentage of Pearls and Inactive Customers was between 95% and 96% — remarkable consistency!

- However, over the four years, the number of Inactive Customers increased steadily from 45.3% to 67.7%, indicating a steady downgrading of Pearls to Inactive customers.

What conclusions can we draw?

- A steady flow of customers is entering the stores but, disappointingly, few stay and an extremely low percentage become Best Customers.

Actually, the number of defections seen is not abnormal among food retailers. As a general rule, companies with many stores have a lower defection rates than companies with only a few, as there are more shopping opportunities available. In this company's case, the majority of new customers, 53.5%, had defected one year later (row 5, col. c). This echoes the results we saw in Figure 9 *(page 41),* which also showed large losses among new customers.

What is remarkable in Table 33 is that over the four years after they first shopped at the chain, the percentage of New Customers becoming Best Customers, ie, 1.2% to 1.6% (row 7), or Key Customers, ie, 4.2% to 4.7% (row 8), didn't change very much at all.

What increased over time were the customers falling by the wayside. In row 5, we see that 45.3% of the New Customers were inactive after one quarter, increasing to 53.5% after one year (four quarters later), to 67.7% after four years. In essence, all of these defections came from the lowest-spending customers, those spending under $25 per week.

The fundamental lesson to take from Table 33 is that there is a steady flow of new customers constantly entering our stores and going through the bother of signing up for our (usually) free loyalty card program. Yet, so many don't return. And so many of those who do, don't make us their primary food store; they drip feed us with a small part of their food budget. This is the challenge for our operators and the rest of the store team: how to provide such a wonderfully differentiated experience that new customers want to return and become significant shoppers with us.

Can management *radically* change the numbers just discussed? Probably not. However, new customer retention and spending improvement programs can, and do, improve such results by a few percentage points. These are some of the incremental yield gains available for your bottom line.

(a)	(b)		(c)	(d)	(e)	(f)	(g)	(h)
Store: Greenville Plaza	Results For Qtr. 1, 2001				Best Customers (BCs) in Previous Qtr.			2,860
	Qtr 1/01..		Week 1	Week 2	Week 3	Week 4	etc.	Week 13
	W/E.		6-Jan	13-Jan	20-Jan	27-Jan	thru >	31-Mar
1	BCs Who Returned to shop, By Week		2,266	2,258	2,315	2,324		
2	BCs Who Returned to Shop, QTD		2,266	2,262	2,280	2,291		
3	**Dept. HHPR**	# Shopped	1,927	1,892	1,950	1,994		
4	Produce Dept.	Week	85%	83.8%	84.2%	85.8%		
5		QTD	85%	84.4%	84.4%	84.7%		
6	**Better (Worse) than LY**	Week	(0.5)%	4.8%	5.6%	1.2%		
7		QTD	(0.5)%	1.4%	4.5%	5.1%		

Read: *(Row 4): Of the BCs who shopped this week, the percentage who shopped this Dept. (eg. 1927/2266 = 85.0%)*

TABLE 34: BEST CUSTOMER HOUSEHOLD PENETRATION RATE

HHPR CREATES BETTER MERCHANTS

One difficulty retail chain store management has is to measure how well each department is really doing. A common measurement used is the sales distribution of each department, eg, the Grocery Department has 52% of store sales, Meat 14%, Produce 9%, etc.

So when a department, say Produce, increases its distribution percentage, is that good? Not necessarily. It may be because bad weather caused shortages and the prices of vegetables have shot up. Or it may be because another department is having problems and its sales and distribution percentages are slipping.

Thanks to customer data, we now have a solution to this measurement difficulty. We can now measure how many of our Best Customers are shopping the department (or any category we wish to measure).

The percentage of Best Customers who shop the department is called the Best Customer Household Penetration Rate (HHPR) of that department.

Best Customers are used for the measurement base because they are high spenders, they visit often, and they have an extremely low defection rate. Thus, any increase or decrease in their departmental purchase habits suggests they are seeing more or less of what they like in the department. Therefore, it's an excellent weekly pulse-taker of a chain's store-by-store departmental performance.

It is best understood by looking at Table 34. This table uses the same Best Customer data as was used in Table 24 *(page 132)*. For example, it tells us that in the previous quarter, the fictional Greenville Plaza store had 2,860 Best Customers (top row, col. h). Of those customers, in the fourth week of this quarter, 2,324 shopped the store (row 1, col. f), and of those who shopped the store 1,994 bought something in Produce (row 3, col. f). This gave the department a Household Penetration Rate (HHPR) of 85.8% (1,994 ÷ 2,324 = 85.8%) (row 4, col. f), which was 1.2% better than the same week last year (row 6, col. f), ie, last year's HHPR was 84.6%.

In like manner, each week's quarter-to-date HHPR and better (worse) performance compared to last year is shown in rows 5 and 7.

Superquinn, ever the thought leader, was one of the first companies to use this concept. Feargal Quinn believes that practically every one of his Best Customers' households will eat at least one Produce item each week. Yet Superquinn's Best Customer Produce Penetration Rates weren't reflecting that. So he ran a special competition for the Produce Departments, with the winners—those with the greatest increase in their penetration rates over the previous year—enjoying a week's trip to the US. After a preliminary test period, to allow the participants to become familiar with how the program and measurements would work, the contest lasted for a quarter, with impressive gains in the Produce Department's HHPRs in every store.

What Superquinn found was that, given the right measurement (and, thus, motivational) tools, departmental managers become even better merchants. The departmental managers challenged their teams to create ways of enticing their Best Customers to shop in their departments on at least one of their visits each week.

There was no end to the creativity of the different teams. They used more sampling and product signage, more nutritional signage, and they introduced more key traffic area displays and cross merchandising. They increased new item promotions and sent more postcards to customers, both informational and promotional. The HHPR focus pushed the store teams beyond the usual "just selling product" mentality. It put them into the shoes of their customer: the position of a true merchant or marketer.

Not only did the company increase—and maintain—its Best Customer Produce Department's HHPR, it also increased its sales to its Potential Best Customers, thereby increasing their allegiance to the department and company and their likelihood of upward mobility.

Another food retailer we have worked with had a wide performance disparity in its Produce Departments and thought it should be achieving better results, so it introduced an HHPR reporting system and started sharing the results with the departmental mangers.

Pure pride and the competitive drive of human beings soon had performances improving as the departmental managers started thinking of ways to attract more of the company's Best Customers to shop more frequently in their departments. After all, "If Terry, a fellow department manager in a nearby store, can get a 94% penetration rate, why can't I?" is the usual human instinct. Store employees love this type of challenge.

Unfortunately, for most businesses worldwide, top management doesn't provide enough challenge, fun, and feedback for employees to make their work exciting. This is one way to do so.

From a practical standpoint, having such interstore contests should be limited to no more than two departments per quarter so that the other departments can help support them with ideas and encouragement and learn from them at the same time.

The same approach can be used, of course, in every company, in every industry. The ratios and departments will be different but the potential for improvement is similar— whether your business is a department store, apparel chain, consumer electronics, or home improvement chain. For example, a home improvement chain, with a lower customer frequency than a food retailer, may select its Promotional and Seasonal Departments to be the first two departments for an HHPR interstore contest. A department store may focus on Women's Apparel and Cosmetics.

Putting the right measurements in front of your operational and marketing teams always leads to better results.

Permanently improving the Best Customer HHPR of your various departments is yet another way of increasing your customer yield and, in turn, your bottom line.

Focus on frequency

It was the English author, G. K. Chesterton, who said: "After seeing something for a hundred times, I see it for the first." I feel that way about frequency, the average number of times a customer visits our stores each week during the course of a quarter (or year). I had piles of information about customer frequency; I just didn't link all the dots together until a few years ago. But now, as I look at customer data "for the hundredth time", it's so obvious how frequency is the primary driver of sales.

For a number of years I was fascinated by Wal-Mart and Kmart putting food items, even milk, in prominent selling positions at the front of their general merchandise stores. Then I saw the warehouse clubs increase their offering of fresh items—produce, bakery, and meat items—and learned that the purpose was to appeal to more customers. Well, it did. But, more importantly, what these companies were doing was encouraging their customers to visit their stores more often by featuring these frequently purchased items. Then I made a fascinating discovery in my clients' customer data. I found, after sorting customers from top to bottom by total spending, that there is a correlation between frequency and spending: *the more frequently a customer shops, the more she spends on each visit.* So not only would these retailers be gaining from their customers' increased frequency, but they would also be gaining from a higher transaction value on each visit as well!

This relationship is seen in Figure 35, a major US food retailer. What we see is that, on average, the top 20% of its customers visited this chain 1.5 times per week over the course of 12 months, spending $35 per visit. This meant that the average top quintile customer spent $52.50 per week (1.5 visits x $35 per visit = $52.50) or $2,730 per year ($52.50 week x 52 weeks = $2,730).

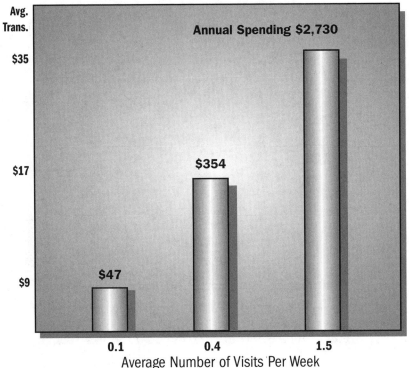

FIGURE 35: FREQUENCY AT MAJOR US FOOD RETAILER

In contrast, the middle quintile of customers visited only 0.4 times a week, spending $17 per visit (ie, $6.80 per week) or $354 per year. And the bottom quintile visited only 0.1 times a week, spending $9 per visit, (ie, $0.90 per week) or $47 per year. The top quintile customers, on average, spent over 50 times as much as the bottom quintile customers did.

What this typical profile tells us is that, on average, our top customers visit us most frequently *and* spend the most on each visit, while our lowest spending customers visit us the least *and* spend the lowest amount per visit. We see that as customer frequency increases, the average transaction size also increases which, in turn, explains the high annual spending of the top quintile.

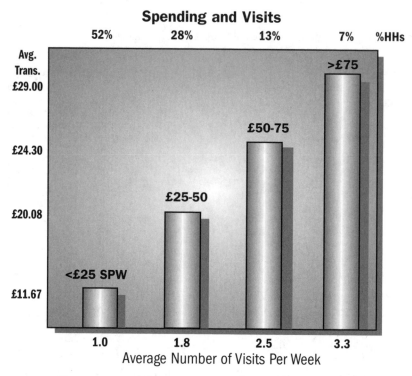

FIGURE 36: FREQUENCY AT MAJOR UK FOOD RETAILER

It can be also be calculated that between 70% and 80% of the total sales gain, between the bottom and middle quintiles, and again between the middle and top quintiles, is due to the increase in frequency. (The other 20% to 30% comes from the increase in the average transaction.)

The most visible way to increase our customers' yield is to encourage them to increase spending—and, as Figure 35 demonstrates, increasing frequency is the best way to do that.

The relationships shown in Figure 35 are common in the United States. However, whenever I talk about them (or any other findings or relationships) in other countries, there is someone who says: "But we are different here!" And so it was with frequency. One UK executive challenged me. He said that he didn't believe that, at his company, the lowest frequency customers would have the lowest transaction value and that the highest spenders would have the highest frequency. By chance, that evening I was going through his company's material and found a table of customers sorted by spending from top to bottom. From that, I was able to prepare for my friendly challenger what we see in Figure 36.

Even though the data covers only one four-week period and it aggregates customers by spending thresholds (eg, 52% of the customers spent under £25 week, while 7% spent over £75 week), the same trend as we saw in Figure 35 held true. At this major UK retailer, as its customers' total spending increased, so did its frequency and average transaction size.

I have yet to find a retailer anywhere in the world where this relationship doesn't hold. Why there's a relationship between how frequently a customer shops and her average transaction size is simple. The more she's in our stores, the more she gets to know all the things we sell and where to find them. Thus, it becomes more convenient for her to satisfy more of her needs when shopping with us.

You will recall from Chapter 1 the *Boomerang Principle*—get the customer to return—which was developed from Feargal Quinn's intuition and experiences. To grow your business, just please the customers and they will come back more often (ie, increase their frequency). Actual customer data, as exemplified in the above two figures, proves that Quinn's intuition was right—over 40 years later. Frequency is indeed the primary driver of sales.

QUALIFYING CHECK-CASHING CUSTOMERS

In the US, in particular, where many customers pay for their purchases by check, customer information is proving very valuable in helping to qualify customers. Should customers' checks be automatically processed at the checkout? If so, for how much in excess of the goods purchased should a customer be permitted to write the check?

Cardholder Segment	Share of Sales %	Share of Bad Checks %
Top 20%	54%	5%
Mid 20%	10%	10%
Bottom 20%	1%	29%
No Card	10%	38%

TABLE 37: BAD CHECK COSTS VS SPENDING LEVELS

It is common among companies with loyalty cards to compare the bad check losses of customers with their different customer spending histories. The analyses have revealed that higher-spending customers incur fewer losses. In other words, your Best Customers are those least likely to bounce checks at your store. Conversely, those shoppers who do not have (or use) a loyalty card have the worst bad check rate, followed by your lowest spending cardholders.

Table 37 is a summary of one company's findings illustrating the point. As customer spending falls from the highest to the lowest levels, the share of bad checks rises quickly. We see that the top 20% of the cardholders of this company generated 54% of the company's total sales, yet accounted for only 5% of the company's bad check loss. In contrast, the bottom 20% of the cardholders, contributing 1% of the sales, account for 29% of the bad check loss. And those who chose not to identify themselves at all (ie, they did not use the company's loyalty card) comprised 10% of the sales and 38% of the bad check loss.

It doesn't take a rocket scientist to figure out corrective policies for the many companies who are confronted with a similar profile. Such companies generally move quickly to change their check cashing policies. They liberalize the check cashing approval procedures for their top customers and tighten procedures for their low spending customers, while applying really stringent procedures for those who have no card member history.

With today's technology, it's easy to have an indicator of each customer's check cashing "grade" appear on a cashier's screen immediately after the customer's loyalty card has been scanned.

QUALIFYING CUSTOMER COMPLAINTS

Since the introduction of loyalty card programs, we have also learned that some of our most frequent and vociferous complainers are low spending customers.

Various CEOs have mentioned to me how happy they are now that, armed with actual customer spending history, they can give more attention, and go to extreme lengths, to please their Best Customers while giving much less attention and priority to their infrequent, low-spending, complaining customers.

For example, one CEO explained to me his company's new hotline procedures. When a customer calls in on the company hotline she is asked to give her loyalty card number. With this, the customer's file is immediately retrieved to check her shopping history, allowing the operator to qualify the company's response.

He continued, saying that the company had recently celebrated its loyalty card's first anniversary. To recognize the occasion, several items were offered to cardholders at dramatically lowered prices, but there was a limit of one item at the low price with each additional $15 of purchases.

It fascinated him to learn that almost all customer complaints to the hotline regarding this limitation were from those who had spent less than $200 in the previous twelve months! Needless to say, no exceptions were made for them. In previous years, he said, exceptions would have been made for such customers as they screamed into the phone describing what "loyal" customers they were!

This differentiated treatment of customers is not new, of course. It's commonplace at airlines, hotels, and banks. It's only new to retailing where customer data has never been previously available.

CHECKOUT SCHEDULING

Another information-rich retailer analyzed his Best Customers' shopping patterns and compared his findings with the scheduling of labor at checkouts. He discovered some mismatches and adjusted his staffing accordingly.

THE BOTTOM LINE

The examples in this chapter amply demonstrate that information is the pot of gold at the end of the loyalty card rainbow. We clearly see that customer information is not just for the marketing department. Rather it is a tool that can improve the productivity or yield of nearly every department in the organization. At the front of the book is a figure summarizing some of its diverse uses. I never cease to be amazed by the power of information that comes from such a simple plastic card!

Dan Lescoe of Big Y summed up so well the situation of those retailers who are rich in customer information. As he told his fellow members at a recent Share Group meeting of global loyalty leaders:

"No matter how much we use our data, we still only have a toe in the water."

PART IV

DRAWING IT ALL TOGETHER

CHAPTER 12: DO LOYALTY PROGRAMS WORK FOR LOW-COST OPERATORS

Who benefits from loyalty programs?

The companies that gain from loyalty card programs are not those with any particular marketing strategy but those with a particular mindset—those who want to understand their customers so that they can run a better business. Low-cost operators are no exception.

CHAPTER 13: KEY SUCCESS FACTORS

What are the essential ingredients of success?

There are six: Commitment. Differentiation. Simplicity. Flexibility. Measurement. Rewards. The global leaders do them well—do you?

DO LOYALTY PROGRAMS WORK FOR LOW-COST OPERATORS

Chapter **12**

The road to success is paved with good information.

... Anon

A simple measure, even imprecise, will go a long way toward getting a company moving in the right direction.

... Tim Koller, author of *Valuation*

We occasionally hear the comment that a loyalty card program isn't for low-cost operators. The rationale offered is that they cannot afford either the cost or complication. In practice, the decision whether a low-cost retailer should run a loyalty program depends on whether or not they will put its customer information to effective, profitable use.

Successful, low-cost retailers with loyalty programs cover a wide range including Every Day Low Price supermarket operators such as Food Lion; hypermarkets such as Carrefour; hard discounters such as Dia; and warehouse clubs such as Costco and SAM'S. This chapter explains how some of them effectively use their customer data.

Dia

Dia, a division of Carrefour, is a highly profitable chain with over 2,500 stores throughout Spain. With more than 10% of the country's food sales, the company enjoys one of the largest market shares in the country. Its stores are small: typically 800 to 2,000 square feet. Its product range is narrow: 800 to 1,000 grocery, perishable, and associated items. Its prices are rock bottom. Its stores are spartan. Management places a fanatical emphasis on productivity and costs.

Nearly all of Dia's stores are in downtown locations. Most customers walk to a nearby Dia store, limiting their transactions to what they can carry home. To encourage new and repeat business, a colorful promotional brochure is distributed every fortnight to the apartments and homes surrounding each store.

In 1997, Dia's CEO, Javier Campo, an astute observer of global retail trends, began wondering whether a loyalty card program would help Dia. Would it even work for his type of operation and his customer segment? Would his customers even bother to carry a card? If they did, what would be more acceptable: a credit card-size card or a key ring card? What would be the more effective program incentive: points, as was already common in Spain and elsewhere in Europe, or two-tier pricing, untried in Europe but common in the US? How could such a program be designed to be compatible with Dia's culture and build upon its strengths to generate increased sales and profits?

Given Dia's unique characteristics and the reality that no other hard discounter in the world had tried loyalty cards before, testing made sense. Management chose a small town with seven of their stores to seek answers to their questions. Because its low-price image was Dia's greatest strength, the company decided that two-tier pricing would be better than points, as lower prices to cardholders would strengthen its price perception in the marketplace.

After observing that most customers carried house or apartment keys, they offered new members a family pack of three cards: one credit card-sized and two small cards suitable for adding to key rings.

Dia launched the test by explaining the new program in its regular brochure, supported by strong in-store signage and information sheets. Stepping up the number of items on the two-tier price program each week, Dia quickly reached a high share of items with two-tier prices: over 20% of its repertoire of 800-1,000 items! These 200+ items comprised all products in its bi-weekly brochure together with items in every store category.

The test was highly successful. So delighted was management with the results that they quickly rolled the program out across the whole Spanish chain. Dia is now doing likewise in their divisions in other countries.

Apart from the marketplace's positive reaction, one element contributing significantly to the program's success was Luis Martinez, head of the program. A mathematician by training, steeped in the company's productivity mindset, he knew that every promotional offer made to cardholders had to yield a return. Both he and Javier Campo also believed that the information gathered could, and should, be used effectively in all parts of the company, from product assortment to real estate.

After several years of trial and success, it was interesting to hear Luis Martinez explain that the greatest information beneficiary of the program has been Dia's real estate department, not the marketing department!

Most customer traffic is walk-in so that, prior to the card's introduction, Dia's knowledge of both its customers' shopping patterns and the distances between their homes and the stores at which they shopped was limited.

Prior to the loyalty card's introduction, real estate personnel interviewed customers at random and then, based on such interviews, estimated the sales volume for any new site under consideration. But now, based on an analysis of actual behavior of customers within 1, 3, and 5-minute walking distances, they can identify new site opportunities with significantly more accuracy and confidence. Given the aggressive expansion plans of Dia, customer information now plays a vital, supportive role in this department.

One byproduct of its narrow product range is that Dia always knows each item's exact gross profit, an exceptional occurrence in the world of retailing. Because of this and the fact that Dia captures over 80% of sales on its *Club Dia* card, the company now knows the profitability of each customer.

This detailed customer knowledge, reinforced by its discovery that the single most important driver of Dia's sales is frequency, has positioned the company well for its next move. It is now making individualized offers to encourage frequency. These offers are made each time a customer shops, and are based upon her purchase and profit history.

As customers complete their transactions at checkouts, the cashier gives them a unique bar-coded offer, valid for several weeks. Dia has found that just as all customers are not equal, all offers are not equal. Based on its past targeting experience, it now matches the appropriate offer to each customer type. This leads to greater repeat business; hence, greater profitability.

This unique Spanish hard discounter has convinced me that a low-cost company can enjoy success with a loyalty program—provided it meshes with the company's culture and that the newfound information is intelligently used to further improve the productivity of all parts of the business.

THE CUSTOMER-CENTRIC CENTURIONS

The warehouse club industry can teach retailers a great deal about how customer information helps steer a business towards success. The two major players, Costco and SAM'S, enjoy annual sales of $60 billion, generated mostly in the US. This high volume industry simply would not exist if there weren't loyalty cards; in their case, paid membership loyalty cards.

Each of these centurions offers around 5,000 stock keeping units (SKUs), compared to 30,000 SKUs for the average US supermarket. Their low-cost, low-margin business is predicated on understanding and satisfying their customers' changing wants and needs. Both capture 100% of their customers' transaction information as no one can shop without presenting a prepaid membership card. Both companies enjoy same-store sales growth.

What's their secret for success? In a nutshell, it's offering such a bundle of value that people are prepared to pay an annual membership fee to get access to it. The clubs then keep adding more value during the year so that members happily renew their $35 to $45 annual membership fees. The formula works extremely well. Both companies have high renewal rates—in the 82% to 86% range—a better result than many retailers that have loyalty cards with no fee at all!

These two membership clubs realize that getting customers to pay up front for the privilege of shopping with them for another 12 months is not only a source of information about past performance, but it's also a great predictor of future sales—and profits. Indeed, over half of the operating profits of each of these two highly successful operators come from their paid-in-advance membership fees! At Costco, for example, in the 12 months ending September 3, 2000, membership fees were almost 52% of profits, as seen in Table 38.

	Millions	
Net Sales (excl. Membership Fees)	$31,621	
Profits before Membership Fees and Taxes	509	48.4%
+ Membership Fees Earned	543	51.6%
= Profits before Taxes	$1,052	100.0%
- Taxes	(421)	
= Profits after Taxes	$631	

Source: Costco Annual Report

TABLE 38: COSTCO'S 2000 SALES AND PROFITS

This up-front fee structure is obviously a crucial part of their business formula. However, both clubs realize that to keep membership fees flowing, their total efforts must be focused on retaining and adding customers by satisfying them—by adding more value to their shopping experience—rather than just advertising to them.

Another key element of their success formula is their 100% customer information capture. They are able to monitor their progress, week by week, through the on-going changes in their customers' behavior with particular emphasis being given to members' frequency and spending per visit. Given the limited number of (SKUs) offered, the calculation of gross profit by customer is relatively easy. These two giants have access to more customer information than any mass retailer today.

SAM'S claims 39 million cardholders, Costco 32 million. The latter has greater total sales, however, because its members spend more. Warehouse club members carry either a Business or Individual membership.

How do these two companies, each with over 30 million members, get over 80% of them to renew their membership each year? By understanding their members and what they buy, then intelligently developing ways to increase the value of being a member.

To paint a broader picture of their customers, one of these clubs has hired outside data houses to append publicly available information to each member's file, including:

- ✪ Demographics (eg, income, race, age, sex, family size, occupation, education)

- ✪ Psychographics (eg, lifestyle, introvert-extrovert, attitudes)

- ✪ Geographics (how far members live from nearest club)

- ✪ Firmographics (if the membership is listed as a business, details such as their SIC code and sales)

With this rich tapestry, buyers can use customer data to understand: (a) who is buying each product; (b) whether they are buying it for home or business; and (c) whether they keep buying it afterwards. With any featured or promoted item, their merchants can learn who bought it, and whether those customers bought it previously and/or subsequently. They are able to develop a clear, composite profile of their customers.

For example, Deborah Grassi, director of research and database marketing at SAM'S, has described its customers as having a median age in the 40's, a median income of $55,000, with 52% of them living less than 10 miles from a club. Their typical membership household comprises 4-5 people with an average net worth of $121,000 (about 70% higher than the US average).

Such customer knowledge is used in the company's decision-making process. For example, after learning the distances members were driving to its club locations, SAM'S found that, by relocating away from low-rent industrial areas and closer to where its members lived, the profits from higher sales more than offset the increased rents. Further, its merchants found that customers who lived over 10 miles from a warehouse buy, not surprisingly, very few frozen food items—prompting SAM'S to develop special packaging to overcome this problem, thereby increasing sales of its frozen products.

Ethnic densities around each club are often plotted, the product mix appropriately refined, and targeted offers are made to these groups inviting them to become members and to buy their preferred items at lower prices.

Individual club product offerings are tailored to member demographics at each location. In Florida, for example, the wine section features boxes and jugs of wine, popular among seniors. Pineapples appear only in clubs with favorable demographics, as do items such as pizza, salad, hot dogs, chicken, and sundaes. A heavy emphasis on using customer data in conjunction with product data is apparent.

With only 5,000 SKUs, they have to ensure that every item is highly productive; and with over half their income coming from annual fees, they have to make every customer feel and experience the value of membership. Neither advertises in newspapers or circulars. Instead they reach out to customers in other ways, such as through supplier-funded targeted mailings.

Knowing the activity of all customers, it's easy for them to identify members whose spending is declining and take corrective action—a better course than inaction and just hoping that members will renew their memberships.

Using profiles of where existing members live, mailings and telephone solicitations to join the club are made to nearby households with similar profiles. To increase members' visitation frequency, both companies have stepped up efforts to include more high-frequency items, especially perishables such as fruit, vegetables, meat, and bakery items.

Marketing analysts study and report on key business indicators, including the acquisition and retention of members, the results of various targeting efforts, the performance of first-year members, new club activity, and comparable club performance. Ad hoc studies on all sorts of customer behavior are frequently initiated. Both companies understand that measuring and monitoring their customer retention rates is all-important.

Even with a qualifying filter in the form of annual membership dues ($45 per year at Costco for business and individual membership; $35 at SAM'S) they have found that not all customers are equal. Some visit frequently; others don't. Some spend a lot; others don't. Some members are significantly more profitable than others.

To add greater value for their higher-spending customers, as well as to build new business opportunities and to minimize defection potential, both have introduced a second level of membership, priced at $100 per year.

SAM'S Elite membership package includes, in addition to regular club benefits, a bundle of benefits that appeal more to individual members, while Costco's Executive membership package favors business members. Participants in these elevated programs are offered a smorgasbord of benefits such as ultra-cheap long distance residential phone calls, check printing and pharmacy prescriptions, a rebate on purchases in higher-margin categories, 24-hour emergency roadside service, and discounted real estate services. Of course, gains from these increased membership fees will allow even sharper pricing on the regular club merchandise, thereby enhancing each club's overall value perception.

In addition to building a stronger relationship with members via these higher-price, value-added memberships, both are broadening their assortment ranges though their website offerings and through supplementary services available to all cardholders, such as discounted travel and auto purchasing. Their approach is similar to what Tesco is doing: they are practicing Agentry, opening up many new buying opportunities on behalf of their members. Both Costco and SAM'S are using the power of their customer databases not only to build their traditional businesses but also to sell more to their high-spending customers via their premium clubs. Their goal is to take a larger share of their members' total spending. They plan to achieve this by adding more services to their off-site product range and strengthen their Internet offering.

These two customer-centric companies are growing their businesses by harnessing the knowledge gained from their customer databases.

THE BOTTOM LINE

There is no question that a low-cost operator, wherever it is based in the world, can cost-effectively gather and use customer information to successfully grow its business. While traditional retailers have shied away from charging anything for their cards, the warehouse club operators have made fees a key element of their business formula. Fees are part of their virtuous success cycle—*Provide great value to show customers that they should become members. Focus on increasing the value to them. Measure your success by your annual renewal rate. Renew your efforts to add even more customer value so that next year the renewal rate will improve yet again.* It's simple but highly effective. All retailers with loyalty programs can learn from this virtuous cycle.

KEY SUCCESS FACTORS

Chapter **13**

Profit in business comes from repeat customers, customers that boast about your product and service, and bring friends with them.
                        ... W. Edward Deming, *Out of the Crisis*

The most difficult thing in the world is to find the simple things.
                        ... Luis Martinez

Throughout this book certain elements stand out as prerequisites for success, both in the First and Second Acts. Using one word to describe each element, the six key success factors can be summarized as follows:

- ◆ Commitment
- ◆ Differentiation
- ◆ Simplicity
- ◆ Flexibility
- ◆ Measurements
- ◆ Rewards

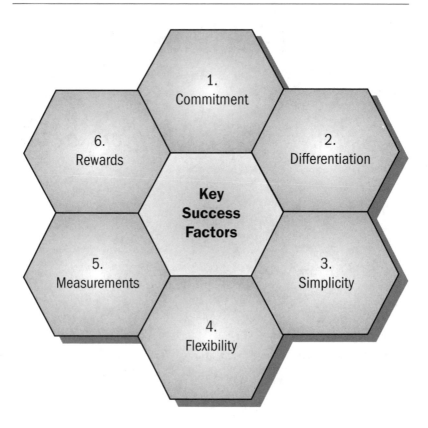

FIGURE 39: THE SIX KEY SUCCESS FACTORS

1. COMMITMENT

Some retailers, when introducing their loyalty program, hand it to the marketing department as a project. The result is seldom a world-class program. Without the commitment and involvement of all departments, disappointment is more likely than success. Commitment means the whole organization is involved with the introduction, execution, and on-going refinement of the loyalty program.

Imagine an airline's frequent flier program if only the marketing staff was involved, but not the check-in staff, gate attendants, and flight attendants. Airline frequent flier programs are successful because they are a seamless part of the whole company.

What does commitment mean? BI-LO, a $3 billion retailer with more than 280 stores in six states, experienced a compelling same-store sales growth of 5% over trend and a profit increase of over 30% in its program launch year—with continued success ever since as a result of the way it approached the launch of the BI-LO BonusCard.

In 1996, Jon Wilken, the company's chief operating officer (who is now CEO), realized the requirements for success. Several years earlier, the company had tested a loyalty program in a handful of stores with the inevitable result: low commitment throughout the organization equaled poor results. This time, with the complete backing of his CEO, Marsh Collins, Jon decided to get the whole organization physically and emotionally involved. Every Friday morning in the eight months prior to the BonusCard's launch in January 1997, Jon chaired a meeting comprising 15 to 20 people representing each part of the organization. Their task was to work through all aspects of the BonusCard program to ensure a successful launch year, a successful First Act.

This weekly meeting signaled to the whole organization that there should be no doubt that the BonusCard was central to the future success of the company and, by implication, every department.

This time, there would be no test in a few stores. Rather, the two-tiered price BonusCard program was to be tested by employees in all stores during the three months prior to launch. Problems encountered and suggestions for improvement from the employees flowed in so that the program launch seemed effortless—yet extremely successful.

Within five weeks of launch, BI-LO's six-page, regular weekly advertisement contained only card-related specials. Sales tracked by the card quickly exceeded 80%. Within eight weeks, 3,000 items (over 10% of their total SKU count) in its stores had two-tiered prices. (Today, that percentage is even higher.) Stores were awash with eye-catching BonusCard shelf signage. All in-store promotional signage unrelated to the BonusCard had been removed. Customers quickly realized that the BonusCard was now an integral part of the BI-LO experience.

The company's commitment to its BonusCard program didn't stop with its launch. The Friday morning meetings continued for another two years as its multi-department team reviewed, refined and developed new programs—and integrated customer information into every part of the business. For example, a key part of its weekly planning process today is a projection of sales of the items planned for the cover page of its weekly circular, using a combination of customer and product information.

BI-LO's continued deep commitment is also reflected in its very high share of sales captured on its BonusCard. Jon Wilken states that the share is now over 90%, providing a very rich database for monitoring its many overt and covert customer-building programs; for minimizing the impact of the many new competitive openings in its marketplace; and for identifying its Best Customers for recognition and rewards. The BI-LO BonusCard program is not just for the marketing department—it is part of the whole organization's ethos. It's almost as though it permeates the company's drinking water!

2. DIFFERENTIATION

Differentiation has two aspects: differentiating the company in the customers' eyes, and differentiating the customers in the company's eyes. A strong loyalty card program plays a vital role in accomplishing both.

To differentiate the company in the customers' eyes, global leaders build their loyalty programs to enhance their existing strengths—they are not "off-the-shelf" programs purchased from a vendor. The program elements and characteristics reflect their unique cultures, adding to the company's positioning in the marketplace. Think of the two retail extremes, Big Y and Dia, discussed earlier. The former, with its large, highly promotional stores and the latter, with stores a fraction of the size of Big Y's, with an extreme, low-cost culture. Both built their loyalty card program elements to reflect and accentuate their very different strengths while using the information to develop their highly differentiated customer offers.

Lettuce Entertain You Enterprises (LEYE) is a company that uses its loyalty card program as a great differentiator of both itself and its customers, as well as acting as a marketing tiebreaker. Founder Rich Melman has built this Chicago-based company, with over 70 units and 34 different formats, each with a distinct character, into a highly successful restaurant chain.

The company's mission is "to offer a multitude of unique restaurant experiences, each marked by exceptional service and the highest quality food." In a month, a Chicagoan could enjoy a different type of meal every night—such as Italian, Greek, Spanish, French, or traditional American fare—and be in a LEYE restaurant.

Diners find that the Frequent Diner program is easy to join. Complete an application form at a restaurant or register on-line at Lettuce Entertain You's website. The $25 entrance fee is refunded in the form of a restaurant reward certificate once the card has been used three times in the enrollment year. Points are earned at all restaurants and on privately catered functions, accruing on a calendar year basis at the rate of one point per dollar spent, excluding tax and tip.

The customer reward structure is classic differentiation. The company is anxious to recognize and reward its high-value members: as soon as $1,000 is spent year-to-date, a Silver Frequent Diner card is sent to replace the member's Blue basic membership card, and a Gold card is sent to replace the Silver when $2,500 is reached. These status cards are valid through the end of the following calendar year. In addition, the Silver card triggers 25% in additional points while the Gold card triggers a 50% bonus. This company is aggressive in rewarding the behavior it seeks.

Lettuce Entertain You loves to recognize its members. In addition to the special recognition "flash factor" that a Silver and Gold card brings, Gold members are accorded priority reservation privileges. Members who have registered their birthdays receive, a few weeks beforehand, a special birthday card entitling them to triple points on the night the member's special event is honored. Simply by presenting the birthday card at the restaurant of choice, bonus points are added when the bill is settled.

Members also regularly receive a newsletter advising of the latest restaurant developments and, if interested, announcements and invitations to attend dinners with guest winemakers and chefs.

Points are converted quarterly into $25 Lettuce Reward Certificates (one for every 250 points), redeemable any night but Saturday. Once members reaches Gold status, they are given a choice of either continuing to automatically receive the Reward Certificates, or to have their points "banked" to be used on some very attractive rewards at higher points levels. For example, a member may redeem 12,000 points for a three-day trip for two to Las Vegas or receive $1,200 in Lettuce certificates. For the ultra Frequent Diner member, 30,000 points can be redeemed for a five-day Super Vacation in the British Virgin Islands! The tiered program is an excellent example of differentiated customer rewards.

The company's program also differentiates its restaurants in its members' minds. Given the very wide choice of restaurants Chicagoans have, a member may decide the type of food she wants but, when selecting, for example, which Italian restaurant to eat at, the potential points together with the chain's consistent quality, often narrow the choice to one of LEYE's four Italian locations. This makes the program a great tiebreaker—and a great example of how a points program can tie together a disparate collection of restaurants into a cohesive whole. Lettuce Entertain You's Frequent Diner program has played a vital role in differentiating the chain in its marketplace.

3. SIMPLICITY

A-Coop, which we read about in Chapter 8, is a great believer in the divinity of simplicity with its highly successful, easy-to-understand, loyalty card program. With no circulars boasting its offers, it relies on quintuple points three fixed days a month as a lure to keep customers coming back. That, along with a few other uncomplicated program features, makes it so easy for customers to understand.

The more a program gets cluttered with options and exceptions, the more it loses its appeal. Some hotel frequent-guest programs, with multiple redemption options, further complicated with both blackout resorts and blackout dates, are guilty of sinning against simplicity as their members get lost in the pages and restrictions.

An easy litmus test of your program's simplicity is to ask a new employee to describe how your program works and what benefits it offers a customer. His response will quickly tell you whether it's simple or complicated.

Simplicity should pervade every part of the program. The application form should have no more detail than what is on your personal check—name, address and phone number—plus, possibly, the number of people in your household. A points program with no expiration date on the points is simpler for the customer than one where points expire 366 days after earning them, as seen in some programs. Programs with qualification periods, such as "spend $400 in the calendar months of January and February" are preferable to "spend $400 in the 8 weeks from January 7 to March 3" because calendar months are easier for customers to remember.

Our customers have so much to remember as it is. If we want them to understand, and then to remember, our program features we must make all elements very simple.

4. FLEXIBILITY

The longer any element of a program stays in place, the more it becomes an expectation—an entitlement—and the more difficult it becomes to make changes without having to offer some costly offsetting alternative. Just as our competitive environment is constantly changing, we need the flexibility to alter, refine, and replace the various parts of our program—indeed, even the program itself—to keep it interesting while minimizing costs. Seldom does any great idea play out forever; it needs to be refreshed. Never are we so lucky that every program we introduce will be highly successful; a ready escape clause, not a straight jacket, should be an integral part of any new program.

We have seen many examples of flexibility throughout this book such as the VIPS card with its rules being changed every two years; the different options available to redeem A-Coop's "P" certificates; the fuzzy value of a point in the SuperClub program; the introduction, and continuation, of Big Y's colored token program with no announcement of who or how one qualifies.

Flexibility is seen in the statement made in SuperClub's highly successful points redemption catalogs that the program is guaranteed to last only 18 months from the date of that catalog, which is issued twice a year. When Green Hills Farms of Syracuse, New York, introduced its card-based donations program, it offered to donate 1% of customers' spending during the first 10 months of the year to the charities of their choice. The two-month break in the program each year gave the company the flexibility to change or cancel the program with minimum disturbance.

Flexibility is seen in the introduction of the Boston-based Stop and Shop "Top Banana" program. The company wanted to provide a vehicle for its store teams and its Best Customers to recognize and know one other. Not knowing how the offer of free coffee, meetings with the manager, and other elements would work, and what would need refining, the company tested it in one store first, to allow itself the flexibility to change or cancel any element of the program, prior to rolling it out to all stores.

We saw cost flexibility at Yoshiya, the Tokyo-based retailer, with its different point rewards on every day of the upcoming month.

BI-LO's Baby Club is another example of flexibility. Rather than follow other retailers who typically offer members a $5 or $10 certificate after every $100 of spending on baby products, the company invites customers with babies to register for a free monthly Baby Club mailer full of relevant information, free gifts and coupons, which are paid for by its baby product suppliers. This approach gives the company enormous latitude in the variety and value of offers made as it is based upon the total purchase profile of the various Baby Club members— a superior approach to the fixed payout method.

While it's heartening to see the continual flow of new programs, prudence suggests that they either be short-term or include an escape clause in case of need. One outstanding loyalty practitioner forgot this when it launched a new program aimed at building both its Best Customer numbers and the size of its average transaction. On top of its existing points program, it introduced a second program—with a different points accumulator and a different name for these new points. It was, to say the least, complicated. Members I spoke to didn't understand the multi-page set of rules and regulations. The new points, with special expiration rules, were earned only above certain transaction thresholds.

Then, because of the length of time involved for members to save enough points to redeem them for something meaningful, the company had no easy way to shut the program down if it wasn't meeting it's objectives. It had allowed itself no escape clause. It could be stuck with a profit-draining dud program for several years, which appears to be the case. The company was absolutely right to be creative and to push the edge of the envelope with its ideas—but it was remiss in that it forgot the vital rules of flexibility and simplicity.

In most sets of principles its common to see two or more of them with some degree of conflict. Our Key Success Factors suffer the same malady, with flexibility frequently conflicting with simplicity.

Consider, for example, "fixed price" stores. One fast growing chain in the late 1980s was One Price Clothing, which sold everything for $6—an amazingly simple concept but extremely inflexible (apart from selling two items for $6). The lack of flexibility meant that as labor, benefits and other costs rose over time (as they always tend to do), margins kept getting squeezed because of the lack of pricing flexibility.

After a few years, the company overcame this problem by raising the price to $7, but the same margin squeeze began again, immediately, at the new price point. Finally, to gain flexibility, the company changed the name on its stores to One Price and More, with no fixed prices, thereby gaining in flexibility but losing in simplicity and its earlier clearly differentiated market position.

The message here is that mastering the combination of flexibility and simplicity should not be undertaken lightly. Neither should it be cavalierly overlooked, for it is the combination that goes to the heart of profitability, both inside and outside of your loyalty program.

5. MEASUREMENTS

Mainline—don't marginalize—your customer data. Don't leave it in the marketing department. That's like leaving store performance data sitting in the accounting department and not getting it to the operators who can use it. Customer information must be turned into on-going measurements to help improve all parts of the business. Customer information is not just something to help develop targeted mailing lists!

The history of measurements runs parallel to, and is deeply intertwined with, the history of business. As David Landes describes in his fascinating book, *The Wealth and Poverty of Nations,* one primary reason why the Industrial Revolution appeared first in Western Europe was its leadership in the evolution of the clock. After the sundial, the first major advance was the invention of the town clock with only one hand, the hour hand. Later came town clocks with both hour and minute hands. Only after that, did clocks appear in the workplace. Each development of the clock—of measuring time—allowed both craftsmen and the nascent factories a more accurate measurement of production. First by the hour, later by the minute. This was a major advance from measuring output by the day, an inconsistent base as it changed according to the varying hours of daylight. A standard fixed time measurement was a better, fairer, and a more motivational standard. As in all human activity, whenever we have been able to develop better forms of measurement, performance improves. Loyalty programs are no different.

Today, now that we have customer information, there are three critical measurements that reflect the current and future health of your business—two of which are pure customer measures.

The three measures are:

a) Operating Profit After Charging for Capital

Operating Profit After Charging for Capital (OPACC) is our Profit before Interest, Taxes, and imputed items (eg, capitalized lease charges and LIFO charges), less our cost of capital (before tax) applied to our net investment (ie, equity plus debt). This pretax variation of what CFOs commonly refer to as Economic Value Added (or EVA™) measures how well we have used our assets over the past 12 months in relationship to their economic cost. It shows whether, during the past 12 months, we have yielded a return greater or lesser than the cost of the net investment involved; it shows whether we have improved or regressed, compared with a year ago. For chain operations, OPACC is best expressed on a *per store, per week* basis.

This metric is the best *lag indicator* (ie, explains what's happened recently) we have of our performance because it shows how effective we have been in using our investment to generate real profits over the past year.

b) Best Customers Per Store

This shows the number of our company's Best Customers divided by the number of stores. (If we have a retail chain that also has a catalog or Internet operation, each of these is treated, initially, as a store for calculation purposes.) This measure is the best *leading indicator* we have available of our overall performance (ie, of what is likely to occur in the near future).

Our Best Customers are, by definition, our highest spending customers. The Best Customer segment, also, as we saw earlier, is that with the lowest defection rate. Thus, the higher this number, the greater the likelihood of excellent sales and profits in the upcoming months.

c) Retention Rate as Key Customers

As discussed in Chapter 8, this metric is the percentage of Key Customers from last year that has remained above the Key Customer spending threshold this year. Using the DROP'N terminology and breakpoints, Key Customers are those who spend $25 or more per week.

If a high percentage of the customers who spent over $25 per week last year exceed that threshold again this year it means that these Key Customers still "love" us, as measured by their pocketbooks. Keep in mind that Key Customers comprise our Best Customers and the customer segment just below them, the Opals (which includes most who have temporarily or permanently fallen out of the Best Customer category), ie, all of our regular customers.

If the Retention Rate is improving, we are doing well in making our core constituency happy and are, therefore, improving the likelihood of increasing our Best Customer numbers. If it's declining, our customers are telling us thatour competitors are offering a more attractive package.

#	Key Business Indicators — Results for Periods Ending Dec. 31		Latest Period (5 wks)			Rolling Quarter (13 wks)			YTD (52 wks)		
			TY	LY	%B(W)	TY	LY	%B(W)	TY	LY	%B(W)
	Cardholder Measures										
1	Card/Total Sales	%	81.2%	81.1%	0.1%	81.0%	81.3%	(0.3)%	81.0%	81.3%	(0.3)%
2	*Retention Rate as Key Customer*	%				77.2%	76.1%	1.1%			
	Best Customers (BC) Per Store										
3	Best Customers (BC) Per Store	#	1,687	1,724	(2.1)%	1,515	1,516	(0.1)%	1,397	1,371	1.9%
4	BC Return Rate (Avg. Per Week)	%	79.9%	80.6%	(0.7)%	77.1%	79.5%	(2.4)%			
5	Best Customers Decline Rate	%	29.2%	28.6%	(0.6)%	26.7%	27.4%	0.7%	28.7%	29.2%	0.5%
6	New Customers Per Trading Week	#	48	42	12.5%	41	40	2.4%	40	38	5.0%
7	**Financial & Non-Financial Measures**										
8	Stores (Weighted Average)	#	104.0	99.0	4.8%	102.0	98.0	3.9%	101.0	96.0	5.0%
9	Transactions Per Trading Week	#k	15.9	16.1	(1.2)%	14.3	14.4	(0.6)%	13.5	13.3	1.3%
10	Items Per Transaction	#	10.5	10.6	(0.5)%	11.1	11.3	(1.8)%	11.2	11.4	(1.9)%
11	Items Per Trading Week	#k	167.7	170.6	(1.7)%	157.9	161.8	(2.5)%	150.6	151.5	(0.6)%
12	Average Selling Price Per Item	$	2.08	1.95	6.5%	2.00	1.87	6.8%	2.00	1.86	6.8%
13	Sales Per Trading Week	$k	349.1	332.2	4.8%	316.1	302.0	4.5%	300.9	281.9	6.3%
14	Gross Profit Per Trading Week	$k	104.7	99.7	4.8%	94.8	90.6	4.5%	90.3	84.6	6.3%
15	Profits Before Tax Per Trading Week	$k	8.7	8.0	8.7%	7.7	7.1	8.4%	7.4	6.7	9.7%
16	*OPACC Per Trading Week*	$k	6.9	6.4	7.6%	6.1	5.5	9.3%	6.4	5.3	17.2%
17	**Productivity Measures**										
18	Items Per Employee Hour	#	40.2	42.7	(6.2)%	41.1	43.7	(6.6)%	41.0	43.6	(6.3)%
19	Store Average Hourly Rate (incl. Benefits)	$	12.97	12.71	(2.0)%	12.66	12.49	(1.3)%	12.48	12.29	(1.6)%
20	Labor Cost (incl. Benefits) Per Item	$	0.32	0.30	(7.7)	0.31	0.29	(7.4)%	0.30	0.28	(7.4)%
21	Overhead Hours Per 100,000 Items Sold	#	66.5	67.5	1.5%	67.7	68.1	0.6%	66.3	68.0	2.7%
22	Net Inventory Days	#	35.2	38.0	8.0%	35.0	39.0	11.4%	35.1	40.0	14.0%

Terms: B(W) % = Better (Worse)%; #k, $k = thousands of items, dollars.   Note: Roundings affect some of the above calculations

TABLE 40: KEY BUSINESS INDICATORS

Other Business Indicators Results for Periods Ending Dec 31		Latest Period (5 wks)			Rolling Quarter (13 wks)			YTD (52 wks)		
		TY	LY	%B(W)	TY	LY	%B(W)	TY	LY	%B(W)
Cardholder Measures										
1 Total Customers Per Store (excl. New)	#	9,562	9,782	(2.2)%	10,960	11,113	(1.4)%	13,944	13,729	1.6%
2 Total Customer Visits Per Week	#	0.96	0.97	(1.3)%	0.73	0.75	(2.3)%	0.48	0.49	(1.6)%
3 Best Customer % of HHs (excl. New)	%	17.6%	17.6%	0.0%	13.8%	13.6%	0.2%	10.0%	10.0%	0.0%
4 New Customers Per Week Addn.Rate	%	0.50%	0.43%	0.07%	0.37%	0.36%	0.01%	0.29%	0.28%	0.01%
5 New Cust. Inactive in Following Qtr.	%				47.9%	50.4%	2.5%			
6 Best Customer YTY Defection Rate	%				3.0%	3.3%	0.3%	1.1%	7.0%	5.9%
7 Key Customer YTY Decline Rate	%				17.0%	16.9%	(0.1)%			
8 Key Customer YTY Defection Rate	%				5.8%	7.0%	1.2%			
9 Total Customer YTY Defection Rate	%				19.2%	18.6%	(0.6)%	17.1%	16.5%	(0.6)%
Financial & Non-Financial Measures										
11 Average Transaction Size	$	21.92	20.60	6.4%	22.16	21.03	5.4%	22.35	21.23	5.3%
12 Earnings Per Share	$	0.04	0.03	34.6%	0.09	0.07	17.6%	0.40	0.32	22.8%
13 **Productivity Measures**										
14 Sales Per Employee Hour	$	83.65	83.06	0.7%	82.18	81.65	0.7%	81.85	81.10	0.9%
15 Store Employee Hours Per Trading Week	$	4,174	4,000	(4.3)%	3,846	3,698	(4.0)%	3,676	3,476	(5.7)%
16 Labor Cost Per Trading Week	$k	54.1	50.8	(6.5)%	48.7	46.2	(5.4)%	45.9	42.7	(7.4)%
17 Payable Days	#	18.2	15.6	16.7%	17.9	15.1	18.5%	17.5	14.9	17.4%

Note: Roundings affect some of the above calculations

Terms: B(W) % = Better (Worse)%; #k; $k = thousands of items, dollars.

TABLE 41: OTHER BUSINESS INDICATORS

The Retention Rate as Key Customers is a vital reading on how our regular customers, on an on-going basis, perceive our offering compared to the alternatives they have.

KEY BUSINESS INDICATORS

An example of a Key Business Indicators Report, together with an optional subsidiary one, is shown in Tables 40 and 41.

The three key measurements just discussed, are key components of these monthly Key Business Indictor Reports. They are the equivalent of Landes' town clocks in medieval Europe and should be highlighted.

The Key Business Indictor Reports are produced by the CFO each month. They identify *all* key business indicators appropriate to the company so that all the vital signs of the company's business health are seen on two sheets of paper.

They include financial, physical and customer data, all relevant in gaining an accurate assessment of the health of the company each month. The indicators may vary from company to company. They may vary within a company over time. The metrics included should all be relatively simple to understand and explain as the reports are, essentially, a monthly x-ray of the whole business. Their purpose is to both show successes and to act as an early warning system of potential problems. They also illustrate how simple it is to mainline key customer measures into the heart of the business in the same way that other non-financial measures have done in the past.

From a different reporting perspective, that of the field operator, an excellent example of a regularly produced management tool is the Customer Business Measures™ Report, developed by Lincoln, Massachusetts-based PreVision Marketing, LLC. This report, slightly modified, is seen in Table 42. It was prepared for a chain of US specialty stores, as reflected in its metrics.

	(a) Division	(b) Company Sales TY/LY%	(c) Retention Rate %	(d) Acquisition New Cust. TY/LY%	(e) Conversion Rate %	(f) Frequency VPW TY/LY%	(g) Upgrade/ Downgrade Gain/Loss %
1	Total Company	2.3%	75.2%	1.1%	35.4%	3.7%	4.5%
2	Denver	10.1%	74.3%	15.3%	35.9%	3.6%	4.5%
3	Dallas	9.2%	75.5%	9.7%	35.3%	3.5%	4.3%
4	Chicago	7.1%	75.1%	7.7%	35.1%	3.3%	4.1%
5	Pittsburgh	6.0%	69.3%	10.1%	31.1%	(0.3)%	2.7%
6	San Francisco	5.3%	77.2%	4.3%	39.2%	3.5%	4.5%
7	Tampa	4.9%	76.1%	3.9%	35.7%	3.4%	4.7%
8	New Orleans	2.1%	75.5%	2.1%	35.5%	3.1%	4.6%
9	Rochester	1.7%	78.3%	0.7%	39.8%	3.7%	4.8%
10	Richmond	1.1%	80.1%	(2.1)%	42.7%	3.8%	4.8%
11	Atlanta	0.5%	71.7%	0.5%	36.1%	3.0%	3.0%
12	Boston	0.4%	75.0%	0.4%	35.1%	2.1%	3.3%

TABLE 42: CUSTOMER BUSINESS MEASURES™ REPORT

Comments: Pittsburgh's sales grpwth, above the company average, is due to its aquisition rate. Yet it has the worst retention rate, frequency change from LY, and upgrad/downgrade measure. In contrast, Richmond has the best retention, frequency and upgrade measures. However, it's having a problem with aquisition, hurting sales growth.

Adapted and reproduced with permission: PreVision Marketing, LLC. Tel: (781)259-5500

In the table, each division's sales growth over last year (col. b) is sorted from highest to lowest. Then (in cols. c to g) it shows the key customer metrics that drive sales.

- How well did each division retain customers from last year?

- Are acquisition rates better or worse than last year?

- How well is each area converting new customers to regular, repeat customers?

- Are customer visits per week better or worse than last year?

- Is the average transaction size up or down from last year?

Such a report allows district and store management to identify where they are doing well and where they need to do better. It is a great example of mainlining customer information for field personnel.

6. REWARDS

Behavior follows rewards is a basic psychological truth. Man is an economic animal in search of self-importance. Therefore, if we really believe that keeping customers is critical to the core of the business, rather than simply paying lip service to the idea, it should be abundantly clear in our internal reward and recognition systems. Unfortunately, this is rarely the case—which leaves the field wide open to those loyalty leaders who are already tying all of this together.

Specifically, relevant customer measurements should be a part of every employee's annual performance appraisal. For employees who are part of a bonus program, some of the critical customer metrics should be included. (We do want a customer-focused organization, don't we?) The ideal bonus program would comprise rewards for improvements in the three key indicators: OPACC, Best Customers Per Store, and the Retention Rate as Key Customers.

Store managers play a pivotal role in attracting and retaining customers through the level of service, quality, and in-stock conditions they offer. One highly successful retailer has changed its store manager bonus from being based solely on the store's profit contribution, to having half based on the profit contribution and the other half on meeting or exceeding the store's historical Best Customer numbers.

We know there is no perfect bonus plan. Typically, bonus plans keep evolving over time. The value weighting given to OPACC, Best Customers, and the Retention Rate of Key Customers will vary according to the evolving financial and competitive position of the company.

How Best Customers are measured for bonus purposes may also vary over time. For example, I have seen different reward values given for last year's Best Customers who, this year, stay at that level versus those who drop to Opal or Pearl. Likewise, different rewards were granted for upgrades to Best Customer level from last year's different lower levels.

In contrast, another company's bonus rewarded just the absolute quarterly numbers of Best Customers.

Yet another creative approach rewards store managers, at the end of each quarter, for the increase in the 13-week average improvement—over the previous year—of customers spending over $35 week in four of the six previous weeks. The focus of this incentive program was on the Best Customer and the near-Best Customer group.

One of the biggest limitations to a successful loyalty program that I've seen on every continent is when a company introduces a loyalty program but doesn't change the way it rewards its employees. It's the age-old folly of rewarding A (the old metrics) but expecting B (the new metrics). Despite all the exhortations of management, if employees keep getting recognized and rewarded for the old measures, while none of the new customer measures are rewarded, that's where priorities are placed. *Behavior follows rewards.*

This is nothing new. Over the decades we've seen many bonus programs of public companies rewarding executives for improvements in reported profits or earnings per share. So that's what they got—but often at the expense of a deteriorating balance sheet. That's why formulae like EVA™ and OPACC are important, as they make an economic trade-off between profits and assets.

If we really want our whole team to become more customer-centric, we must incorporate appropriate customer metrics into our employee evaluation and bonus programs. Otherwise, we are simply wishing for one result but rewarding another—a sure sign of business schizophrenia!

CLOSING THOUGHTS

The distinguishing characteristic of the Second Act is how customer information, applied intelligently throughout the whole organization, can improve both our customer relationships and our corporate results.

The differentiating characteristic of companies having a great Second Act is that they practice the six Key Success Factors, albeit at varying levels.

Obviously, there will be a Third Act. The best always find ways to improve. However, before that script is written, there is still so much to be done honing our Second Act and keeping our customers in their seats.

I hope that the examples, ideas and practices in this book have been helpful and play a part in your "show's" future success.

Good scripting, good planning and good luck!

LIST OF FIGURES & TABLES

INDEX

A

B

C

ABOUT THE AUTHOR

Brian Woolf is one of the global leaders in loyalty marketing. The author of two definitive works on the subject, *Measured Marketing: A Tool to Shape Food Store Strategy* and *Customer Specific Marketing,* he has, since 1993, been assisting retailers develop and strengthen their loyalty programs. The techniques and metrics that he has developed and taught have become guiding principles for those operating some of the leading loyalty programs in the world today.

He is the President of the Retail Strategy Center, Greenville, South Carolina, whose global clients cover the full range of retailing: from hard discounters to hypermarkets; from self-service to high-service supermarkets; from small retailers to global chains. Brian is also a frequent speaker at conferences in the US, Europe and Japan.

His whole business life has been immersed in retailing. Prior to his total commitment to loyalty marketing in 1993, his corporate roles include being Deputy Managing Director of Progressive Enterprises (Foodtown), a major New Zealand retailer; Chief Financial Officer of Food Lion, a leading US food retailer; and President of One Price Clothing, a women's discount apparel chain. He has an M.Com. (Economics) from Auckland University, New Zealand, and an MBA from the Harvard Business School.

He may be contacted at:

Retail Strategy Center, Inc.
6 Parkins Lake Court,
Greenville, South Carolina 29607-3628, USA

Tel: (864) 458-8277   *Eml:* bpw@brianwoolf.com
Website: http://www.brianwoolf.com

SPECIAL ORDER FORM

Books by Brian Woolf

Please copy and fax to (USA) +609-347-2455
Raphel Marketing, 118 S. Newton Place, Atlantic City, NJ 08401
Tel: (609) 348-6646   Toll-free: (877) 386-5925   Eml: info@raphel.com

 # copies   **Total**

____   *Loyalty Marketing: The Second Act*   @ *$29.95*   _____
____   *Customer Specific Marketing*   @ *$29.95*   _____
____   *Shrinking The Corporate Waistline*   @ *$14.95*   _____

Plus Postage/Handling $4.00

Total $_____

Please send to:

(Name)_____

(Company) _____

(Street Address) _____

(City)_____ (St.) _____(Zip)_____

(Country)_____ (Tel): (   ) _____

Credit Card: *(check one)* ❏ Visa   ❏ MCC   ❏ American Express

Account #: _____ Expires: _____

Cardholder Signature _____

Quantity discounts available. Please call for information.